THE
TRIP
BEYOND

THE
TRIP
BEYOND

by *Brian Ruud*
with
Walter Wagner.

PRENTICE-HALL, INC.
Englewood Cliffs, N.J.

The Trip Beyond
By Brian Ruud With Walter Wagner
Copyright © 1972 by Brian Ruud and Walter Wagner
All rights reserved. No part of this book may be
reproduced in any form or by any means, except
for the inclusion of brief quotations in a review,
without permission in writing from the publisher.
Printed in the United States of America
Prentice-Hall International, Inc., London
Prentice-Hall of Australia, Pty. Ltd., North Sydney
Prentice-Hall of Canada, Ltd., Toronto
Prentice-Hall of India Private Ltd., New Delhi
Prentice-Hall of Japan, Inc., Tokyo

Library of Congress Cataloging in Publication Data
Ruud, Brian, Date
    The trip beyond.
    Autobiography.
    1. Conversion. I. Wagner, Walter, Date
II. Title.
BV4935.R76A3   248'.24   72-3720
ISBN 0-13-930958-6

Second Printing........October, 1972

For Mom and Dad

Special appreciation to my wife, Gayle,
whose encouragement and long hours made
this book a dream fulfilled.

"There are many fine women in the world,
but you are the best of them all."

PROVERBS 31:29

Contents

*I love the Lord, because he hath heard my
voice and my supplications.
Because he hath inclined his ear unto me,
therefore will I call upon him as long
as I live.*
—Psalms 116:1–2

THE
TRIP
BEYOND

1

The Commandment Killer

For the wages of sin is death.

ROMANS 6:23

Suicide was going to be my next trip.

Already I was half dead and all but buried in the subterranean pit of Canada's San Quentin, a slag heap of broken men, a mean pile of brick and steel called Prince Albert Prison, located in my native province of Saskatchewan.

BRIAN RUUD SUICIDE. I could visualize the headline in my hometown paper, the Saskatoon *Star-Phoenix*. Over the last several fleeting, furious years, it had chronicled my long list of offenses against God and man.

No one would be surprised at my death. Everyone, my family included, would agree that my suicide was the inevitable climax of an angry, misbegotten, useless life. I wasn't filled with self-pity or paranoia, but I couldn't think of a single person who would miss me. At my funeral, Mom, Dad, my two sisters and brother would mourn me, but more with resignation than regret.

I had no redeeming quality, no excuse for living. Taking my life would be doing everyone, especially myself, a favor.

1

I was shambling along the deep-lock corridor at the bottom of the prison between two guards—headed for the Hole.

In contrast to my lonely, self-declared last-mile walk, above me there was an institution in motion—four hundred and fifty cons who, compared with the rigors of solitary confinement, were living in luxury. I'd been told what to expect in the Hole. Nevertheless, I was impatient to get there, eager for the final super-cool blackout that would end all the hassle.

Soon I'd be just another of the approximately one thousand people who kill themselves every day. Each year some 365,000 (more than three times the population of Saskatoon) men, women, students, and kids as young as ten choose death instead of life. My initial horror had trailed off since reading that statistic. Now I could understand the feelings of those lucky 365,000. Adding it up, life was a bummer, and death would be a new high. I was looking forward to death the way I had anticipated Christmas when I was a child.

Though I had no specific plan at the moment, I knew it wouldn't be difficult to find a way of killing myself. All it took was a touch of ingenuity, and I had as much inventiveness as a number of other cons who'd successfully committed suicide. One had tied a television cord to the vent in his cell, strung the other end around his neck, climbed on his bunk, and let himself drop. Several had concluded their sentences with an overdose of barbiturates, smuggled in to them, for a price, by other cons or the guards. The most bizarre case involved a lifer who choked himself to death by stuffing the pages of a book into his mouth. The book he had used was the Bible!

The corridor was damp and cold. A chill spread along my spine, then infiltrated every part of my body. Besides my shivering, I felt wan and weak, close to collapse.

One of the guards suddenly called a halt. He was a burly man in his forties, rheumy-eyed and beer-bellied. "Ruud, this is where you'll be next," he said. For some reason there was a smile on his face.

Looking around I saw six gaily painted cell doors, each a different color—yellow, green, pink, orange, blue, and red. Amidst the prison's unrelenting, metallic gray, the swim of bright hue was completely unlikely, totally incongruous.

"Death Row!" the still-smiling guard added before I could ask for an explanation. "The colored doors add a bit of cheerfulness for the condemned men. The government does what it can to brighten things up while the boys are waiting."

It struck me as a sour, ironic joke. Perhaps the splash of color did help relieve the otherwise drab surroundings of those sentenced to die. But I doubted it.

I wanted to go on, still impatient to snuff out my life. Right now I had little interest in Death Row. It was a drag, it would take too long to die there. The guard was enjoying himself, however. He opened the cell with the yellow door. It was furnished with a table, chair, and a large mirror.

"When they bring you in here," he said with the enthusiasm of a bus tour conductor, "you'll eat your last meal—steak or whatever you like—at that table, just before your hanging. You'll have silverware and ordinary dishes and all the cigarettes you want. You'll even get a new suit, so you can go out in style.

"I've been here a long while, and watched a lot of them go. They usually act the same way. They take a long time eating that final meal. Then they smoke and pace their cells. Every few minutes, they call out asking for the time. When the clock finally strikes the hour, they comb their hair in the mirror and look at themselves for the last time."

My curiosity was finally aroused. "Then what happens?" I asked.

"Be glad to show you."

We walked several yards further down the corridor. The guard swung open a large steel door at the end of the cell block and invited me in. I stepped into what seemed more a vault than a cell, dark and eerie.

"Now," he said, with a smirk of laughter, "you're standing on what happens."

Peering down, I saw my feet had come to rest on a shiny steel plate flush with the cement floor.

"Our gallows," the guard announced merrily. "Nothing as

3

romantic as thirteen steps and a blindfold, but just as efficient."

He went to a small switchboard banked against the far wall.

"One press of this button, and that trap door under you ends your misery."

I almost shouted for him to hit the button. *Get on with it, man,* I nearly screamed. *You're right, I want my misery ended.*

"Look up," he said.

Overhead was a sleek steel beam, strongly braced. There were still strands of rope on it, a souvenir from the last dude whose neck was stretched.

Back in the corridor we went on for several yards, then made a sharp left turn to another block of cells—unpainted and uninviting.

"Here's the Hole," the other guard said, speaking for the first time. There was far more kindness in his tone.

I was shoved into one of the cages. By no stretch of the imagination could it be called a cell.

"All right, punk, take off your clothes," the burly guard commanded.

I stripped as fast as I could, a slow and painful process because every muscle ached. With practiced eyes and hands, the two of them went over my body and clothes, looking for concealed weapons. They found nothing. "Sorry, Ruud," the young guard said tersely, the kind tone still in his voice. It was small comfort. They left, slamming and bolting the door.

The world had finally locked me up and thrown away the key. But I wouldn't be in solitary long. Sooner than anyone expected I'd be out—on a stretcher.

I put on my shorts and pants. I was naked from the waist up. Despite the cold and the gummy dampness of the Prince Albert tomb, despite my obvious, uncontrollable shivering, they had taken my shirt and shoes, because suicide, or attempted suicide, was no random occurrence in the Hole. The shirt was confiscated as a precaution against my tearing it into rectangular strips and stringing a rope together; the shoes so I couldn't remove the nails from the heels and use them as possibly lethal instruments.

4

I was grateful for one thing—that there was no mirror in the Hole. I didn't want to look at myself.

I was only too aware of my appearance. I weighed 118 pounds, forty-seven pounds below my normal weight of 165. My shoulder blades were ready to burst through my skin. There were pimples on my face, sores and welts all over my body. My eyes were sunken shafts, my lips chapped and dry, my hair disheveled. My throat felt raw, and I was sure the inside of my mouth was bleeding. From head to toe I was a wreck, a disgrace to the human race. And since I was more animal than man, fittingly, I had been thrown into a cage.

The cell from which I had just been removed in the upper part of the prison was a penthouse compared with what I had now. My regular cell had been fairly roomy. There I had a cot, blankets, sheets, a sink, a small cupboard for personal possessions. There I was allowed cigarettes, books, magazines, knives, forks, plates, pencils, and paper. None of those amenities were allowed in the Hole. The cage didn't even have a mattress, much less a blanket. Aside from a toilet, there wasn't any utilitarian comfort or evidence of civilization.

Painful though it was, I extended my hands and touched both walls. There was still an arm span left over. The bars of the tiny, windowless dungeon were a scant three inches apart. Outside my cage a high-wattage, naked bulb cast a steady glare of light. It would be impossible to tell night from day. Permeating everything was the sickening smell of prison, a combination of disinfectant, urine, the stench of unwashed bodies and septic tanks.

"Anybody here?" I shouted through the bars.

Silence echoed back. I had the pit of the prison all to myself. I was the king of the prison's graveyard, king of the terrible enclosures, six in nearby Death Row and the six used for solitary.

I continued shouting to see if a guard would come if I kept it up long enough. Ten minutes later, all was still silence. I didn't know how often, if ever, the guards made their rounds. Maybe they never came by.

No, the Hole was escape-proof, except if you went out as a

corpse, but there was nothing in my cage I could use to destroy myself. Only condemned cons were permitted a television set with that beautiful cord. I had no pills and no money to buy them. If that younger, kinder guard came around, maybe I could con him into sneaking me forty or fifty barbiturates. I had built up so much resistance to drugs, it would take that many downers to do the job. I decided definitely against one mode of suicide, though. Even in the Hole, I had some shred of dignity left. I wouldn't lower myself to ask for a Bible, a Book that only hypocrites pretended to live by.

I slumped down against the bars, physically and mentally exhausted, and drifted off to sleep for a few hours. When I awoke, I was hallucinating, one of the lingering symptoms of too many drugs for too many years. On my knees I rattled the bars, crying with honest fear as I saw bright red flames. "It's burning! It's burning! My God, the prison's burning down! Let me out! Let me out of here!"

No answer, nothingness. I was in a virtually airtight vacuum, ignored, forgotten, abandoned, discarded, in a vise of steel and concrete. Man, why couldn't they supply a cyanide pill to cons who wanted one? In my case, cyanide would be a cheap and practical way out for the Province. I'd cost the taxpayers a fortune in stolen loot, plus thousands of dollars in police time, court expenses, and imprisonment. How many thousands more would it cost if I was convicted—as I was certain I would be—of the three serious charges facing me, offenses that carried total penalties of thirty years?

The hallucination had faded away, and I was confronted with boredom as solid and thick as the walls of my steel cave. Nothing to do, nothing at all. I'd always been hyperactive, with more adrenalin than any one person had a right to. Normally, I was a bundle of energy and nerves, incapable of sitting still, whether or not I was popping pills. I had to have *something* to think about.

But what?

Think, man, think. Think about thinking. Think about anything in this rotten world to keep your sanity. Otherwise you're going to be carried out of the Hole in a straitjacket instead of a stretcher.

One thought finally invaded the void of my mind. But it was a bummer, the last thing I wanted to focus on. I tried dismissing it . . . yet it persisted. Of all the images, ideas, and possibilities under the sun, I found myself captured in the contemplation of the Ten Commandments.

That was bad news. I wasn't anxious to wrestle with that nonsense about Moses, who supposedly was given God's laws a couple of thousand years ago. That's how preachers, those religious phonies, snared you—made you feel guilty, made you feel that because some dude named Adam and a chick called Eve committed original sin in the Garden of Eden, everybody had to carry the burden.

It was a bad scene, and I wanted no part of it. I was already carrying guilt enough. Nobody had to tell me I was as much a sinner as Judas. Hard as I tried to rivet my attention elsewhere, anywhere, the thought of the Commandments continued to scud through my brain like winter storm clouds over Saskatoon.

Okay, cool. If it had to be, I'd groove on the Commandments. What could I lose? I was so far down there wasn't a ladder long enough for me to climb out. And at least it was better than nothing. Though I hadn't given a thought to any of them in years, to my amazement I discovered I could recall them all from Sunday School lessons pounded into me during my youth. They clicked through my brain like slides moving through a projector.

Thou shalt have no other gods before me . . .

So far as I was concerned, God was a myth and religion a racket. I didn't know who or what God was, and I'd seen no convincing, lasting proof in my life that God existed. In my mind there was no God. I ought to know . . . since I was the son of a minister! My father had spent most of his adult years as a preacher, putting God and his church above everything else. But that was his trip, not mine.

If I had a god, it was Satan. I'd paid my dues to him over and over, I'd worshipped him to the exclusion of that imaginary white-bearded, temperamental, jealous old Man on His golden

7

throne in heaven. He was supposed to be a God of love and kindness, who brought you peace and serenity, who put everything together—but He hadn't done any of that for me.

The only rewards, the only kicks, the only highs. I'd ever received were shoveled out by the pitchfork of the Devil. And I carried my tithes and offerings to him in abundance, given him more than money, given him my heart and soul and mind. I'd sold out to him completely. No mistake about it, and nothing in the world would ever make me change my allegiance.

Thou shalt not make unto thee any graven image . . .

Heavy, man. My graven images were a set of burglar's tools and a ring of a hundred passkeys that would flip any lock from Vancouver to Florida, from Quebec to California. My idols were the knife and the gun, speed and booze. One of my most cherished idols was a souped-up sedan that burned rubber at 120 m.p.h. On one occasion, it had outdistanced a siren-blasting police car that was chasing me.

Al Capone was my patron saint, which was perfectly natural for a kid who'd spent practically all his time in a section of Saskatoon that was aptly known as Little Chicago.

My other heroes were a bunch of hoodlums, notably a sharp dude named Alex Cordova. Everyone said Alex had ties to the Detroit branch of the Mafia. I believed it. For a long time, Alex Cordova had been my idol and best friend . . . until he came at me with a butcher knife, nearly killing me.

Thou shalt not take the name of the Lord thy God in vain . . .

More times than I could count, I'd cursed God and Jesus.

My father had howled Jesus at me before I was out of diapers. But Jesus was nothing but an ancient hippie, another dude with a beard who lived back in the days of the Bible.

All I knew about Him was that He was a hotshot preacher who'd been busted and walked His last mile up some hill, walked the same last mile as cons in Prince Albert's Death Row. That much about Him was cool.

But what good did all His preaching do? What did He have to do with me? Where was Jesus when I needed Him? The world was still in a mess. I was in a mess. The hell with God, the hell with Jesus. Their action was for squares.

Remember the Sabbath day, to keep it holy . . .

What the God-fearing called the holy Sabbath was the only commandment that was a blessing. For me, Sunday was just another day to get stoned or drunk. Its one major advantage was that it was easier to break into private homes, appliance stores, jewelry shops, and especially drugstores to scoop their shelves of pills. The perfect time to hit all those straights was when they were in church, listening to that religious swill. Let Jesus help them when they came back and found themselves robbed blind. I planned as many capers as possible for Sunday.

Honor thy father and thy mother . . .

That was anything but a commandment to me. It was a joke. I had paid no honor to my parents, and I didn't think they deserved much.

My father had been a damn fool. He'd quit a $25.000-a-year job as Canada's western regional manager for the Electro-Lux Vacuum Cleaner Co. That was heavy bread. Who but a damn fool would kick it away for a collection plate, a humiliating beggar's bowl that never produced any real money?

He'd become a Pentecostal preacher, the Holiest Roller anywhere in Canada or the States. When he preached, the wrath of God thundered, and fire and brimstone flashed. He'd had a tough struggle building his ministry, starting as a circuit rider, establishing a string of churches in backwater towns and living the hardscrabble life of a traveling evangelist. Later he had built a church in Saskatoon which now, thanks to me, was down at the heels, almost empty, almost destroyed. I couldn't see where all his struggles added up to anything of value.

And now that I was in trouble again, he wouldn't even stick by me. A few days before, I'd been allowed to phone home from the prison.

"Hello, Dad? Brian . . ."

I never got to say another word. The line throbbed with his tears and rage.

"I've been praying for you," Dad said. "I've spent thousands of dollars on lawyers because you chose crime. drugs, horror, prison. I've loved you and tried every way I could to help. I may have failed in the task. But I've done my best in trying to make

9

up for my failure. It seems that whatever I've done hasn't helped. There's nothing more I can do. Brian, you have just about destroyed my life. You've ruined my church, our family, our name. You've almost killed your mother. I can't take it anymore. So it's all over. I'm turning my back on you. I've prayed my last prayer for you. I'm going to forget that you were ever my son. You've chosen your own road to walk. Now you've got to walk it alone."

Then he hung up, and I still felt bitter. I figured honor was a two-way street. If a son was supposed to honor his father, why shouldn't a father honor his son? It didn't occur to me that I had provoked him to the breaking point.

While there had been much calculated and involuntary rebellion, insult, and resentment in my attitude toward Dad, that wasn't true with Mom. I was always closer to my mother than my father, but I had rendered her precious little homage. I had tried in my own way to pay her honor and give her love and respect, but somehow it had never worked, maybe because I cursed her so often and argued with her so frequently when she demanded obedience and discipline or chewed me out after learning of my law-breaking escapades. She was less bombastic and showy than Dad, but Mom was also a turned-on Christian and had been most of her life. But it hadn't seemed to calm the waters of her often troubled soul, most of her grief brought on by me. Actually, she didn't know a tenth of what I'd done, which was just as well. Twisted and illogical though it was, my principal demonstration of love for Mom was sparing her all the gritty, grimy details of my criminal activities.

When it came to morality and plain simple decency, my brother and sisters were saints when matched against her youngest child, her runt son who'd been running amok for reasons that no one in our family could fully fathom.

After Dad's savings were tossed down the rat hole of his church, Mom took a job as a pastry cook in a downtown hotel. Her shift began at five o'clock in the morning, and, standing on her feet, she worked like a mule for long hours and little pay.

In the last few years she had spent countless hours in bed, close to a nervous breakdown, so ill in spirit she rarely ate except

10

when a member of the family, a friend or neighbor brought food and forced or cajoled her into taking a little nourishment.

Mom could pray up a storm and she had always prayed for me. Undoubtedly she was praying this moment for her black sheep offspring. But if there was a God, He never listened or answered her supplications. Anyway, prayer wasn't about to get me out of the Hole.

Honoring your father and mother might be a noble idea scrawled in the Bible, but experience had taught me that it wasn't very practical. Long before the term became a fashionable cliché, there was a generation gap between my parents and me that yawned as wide as the Grand Canyon. But that was their fault. I didn't ask to be born.

Thou shalt not kill . . .

Apparently I was committing slow homicide against my mother and probably my father as well, but never during my crime spree had I straight-out killed anyone.

Not that I wasn't capable of murder. Even now, under the right circumstances, I wouldn't hesitate a second. I'd played with the notion often, and figured that a carefully planned and executed murder was the easiest crime to commit and get away with scot-free, particularly if you arranged the killing so that there would be no witnesses.

Several times, I'd been surprised by frightened housewives who'd stumbled on me while I was looting their homes. I always carried my .32 caliber as protection against the heat on these capers because it seemed the tough, manly thing to do. On such occasions, I'd head for the nearest door or window. It seemed cowardly to murder a helpless woman, but if I was caught by the cops, I was certain I had the guts to shoot it out with them.

The fact that I hadn't yet killed was mere accident, pure chance. But now I was going to remedy that, and finally add murder to my catalog of crime. The victim, of course, would be myself.

Thou shalt not commit adultery . . .

I didn't know many straight people, but I was aware that practically any of those allegedly God-fearing, churchgoing, Lordtithing straights would indulge in adultery every chance they got, women as well as the men.

Few, if any, married dudes would pass up the opportunity to make it with chicks other than their wives. They'd ball their secretaries, pick up an accommodating waitress or bar girl. And they'd gladly pay for a prostitute. I'd done my share in helping adultery along. I'd had a small stable of young, wild, stoned-out chicks hustling for me. Most of the lust-loined who supported our small but busy prostitution ring were married businessmen from the most respectable sections of town. The remainder of our clientele were primarily from Saskatoon's Chinese colony.

In my own neighborhood there were at least half a dozen bored housewives, most of them booze freaks, who'd pile into bed with anything that wore pants, from the milkman to their husband's best friend. The only couple I was certain hadn't participated in adultery was my Mom and Dad. I had to give them that much.

Thou shalt not steal . . .

I'd turned thief at the age of five. In the ensuing years I'd been arrested on ten charges, appearing in court nearly as often as a judge. I was so intimate with that scene that several times I'd acted as my own lawyer. Among other things, I'd been busted for rape, dangerous driving, breaking and entering, theft, obstructing a peace officer, possession of stolen property, drug possession, and entering a dwelling with intent. Added up, I probably owed the government at least two hundred years in prison if I confessed to every caper—which was impossible. There'd been so many I'd forgotten all but the biggest scores and the ones on which I'd been brought to trial. Nor had I flinched from stealing the offerings from my dad's church.

Thou shalt not bear false witness against thy neighbor . . .

I was a born liar. I'd lied to my folks, to the police, to myself. To avoid being found guilty in one of my court cases, I'd paid off friends to commit perjury. I was generally so stoned that I could seldom tell the difference between lies and the truth.

But who cared? What difference did it make? The whole stinking world was a lie.

12

Thou shalt not covet . . . anything that is thy neighbor's . . .

Besides my other achievements as a thief, I was one of Canada's ranking heel-and-toe caper men—stealthily entering motel rooms during the day while tourists were out on the town or late at night while they were sleeping. I'd lift all the cash and valuables I could find.

I had coveted the few coins and an occasional dollar bill stolen from the puke-stained clothes of drunks I'd rolled. I'd also stooped on occasion to stealing cheap bottles of muscatel from winos. I had coveted the money I received from illegal—and crooked—gambling games that I'd banked, had coveted the cash that came to me from everything I'd scooped. How else could I support a drug habit that cost hundreds of dollars a month?

Ten tries, ten strikes. Brian Ruud, the 19-year-old son of a minister . . . Commandment Killer *par excellence.* I'd violated every one of them—in spades.

Having run through the Commandment trip, I had to decide what to think about next. *Stir crazy* wasn't an idle term, and I wanted to **keep** my sanity for the one important thing I still had to do on **earth.**

I heard a sudden, scratching sound and saw a tray being slipped into my cage through a slot at the bottom of the bars—dinner. Or was it breakfast, or lunch? By now I had completely lost track of time.

There were three pills on the tray. Unfortunately, they weren't uppers or downers—I was ready to space out high or low. Unfortunately, not one was cyanide. Just vitamins, nesting beside a bowl of soup. But also on the tray, gleaming dully, was a cheap aluminum spoon.

There it was—my escape from the Hole!

I didn't bother with the vitamins or the soup, but grabbed the spoon and tried to twist the bowl from the handle. Once I could have done it in a minute with one hand, but now I hadn't enough strength. I inserted the spoon between two of the bars,

13

working it back and forth. It took about ten minutes to sever the handle.

Now I had a weapon, somewhat blunt, but maybe pointed enough to do its job. With all the force I could gather, I jabbed the spoon handle into my left wrist, hoping to see an artery gush blood. It was too blunt. There wasn't even a hint of a skin puncture.

But the spoon handle was still my ticket out.

Methodically, I began to hone it to a sharp point against the floor. Slow . . . slow . . . but the tiny shavings were wearing off . . . it was coming along nicely. Soon it would be sharp enough.

Since I was a condemned man who wasn't eating a last luxurious meal I allowed myself two final wishes. They would seem exotic and deranged to others, but I was dead serious about them.

First, I wished that my mother would pray for my death instead of my deliverance from prison. I'd read that in pre-Christian Hawaii and in the modern-day West Indies, people were literally prayed to death through voodoo. It was a way of getting rid of enemies. And if the victim believed in the strange rite, he invariably would be dead in ten days. If Mom was being honest with herself, she must realize by now I was her enemy.

Pray, Mom, pray me happy . . . pray me dead.

My second wish—and I cursed because nobody would ever know it—was to have my headstone inscribed exactly the same as Capone's.

QUI RIPOSA

BRIAN DOUGLAS RUUD

BORN: JUNE 26, 1946

DIED: NOVEMBER 24, 1965

Man, wouldn't that blow everybody's mind? *Rest in peace, Ruud, you pill-popping, thieving, miserable, God-hating disgrace to humanity.*

14

Death now was so close I could taste it. In a little while, I was going to be free. And I was going to shake hands with the Devil. Headed straight for hell, it would be my last trip, and I knew the territory well.

As I patiently continued scraping the spoon to a knife-edge, it occurred to me that I'd been in hell for as long as I could remember.

2

Registration of a Live Birth

O my son Absalom, O Absalom,
my son, my son!

II SAMUEL 19:4

Not every kid can boast that he came within a hair-breadth of becoming a killer at kindergarten age.

Before the incident that was to involve me in a near-murder, I'd already rejected my father's scene. Barely out of diapers, I thought I wanted to follow his footsteps in the ministry. Since I hadn't yet had an opportunity to compare careers, the choice was natural and obvious, fortified by Dad's encouragement. On the rare occasions when he was home, Dad would bounce me on his knee. "My preacher son," he'd say. In the eyes of my folks I was already ordained. They made a home movie of me in a red jumpsuit, clasping a New Testament, mugging, prancing, clapping, shouting, and dancing for the Lord, a lilliputian Holy Roller.

But when I tried preaching to my friends, the reception was

17

far less enthusiastic. My infantile sermons brought laughter and scorn. By the time I was five, I had reached the conclusion that preaching was a drag. It was nowhere, not nearly as exciting as the budding careers of my playmates who wanted to be the Lone Ranger, Mounties, firemen, and hockey players. But there was one occupation none of them had chosen. I had it all to myself.

"When I grow up," I declared, "I'm going to be a gangster."

I said it simply for shock and attention. But to prove I meant it, I led a four-member junior cabal on a foray to a dime store where we stole rubber knives.

"Let's stab somebody," I challenged.

We hid behind a fence a short distance from my house and waited for a victim. A young mother, pushing her baby in a carriage, approached our ambuscade. When they reached us, I ordered the attack, snarling in my toughest voice, "Let's go!"

We scrambled over the fence, surrounding our prey, our rubber knives falling harmlessly against the carriage. The mother was outraged nevertheless, but we paid no heed to her screams and were indifferent to the supine, sleeping child.

The woman's anger only goaded me on. I decided to give her a first-class reason for making a fuss. It was okay for my buddies to have those dinky rubber knives, but since I was the leader of the gang, I rated special equipment. And I had to prove how tough I was. I ran into my house, rummaged through my brother Dave's Boy Scout gear and found his hunting knife.

When I reached the street again, my pals were still harassing the woman and the baby with their toy shivs. With my real knife, it was up to me to inflict the *coup de grace.*

I raised my hand and with a vicious swipe my weapon tore through the thin leather umbrella. The knife imbedded itself into the pillow—less than an inch from the baby's soft skull.

The woman grabbed the child up into her arms. Choleric, she spit indignation and venom at me. "You're a preacher's son! Is that what your father teaches you? How to stab, how to kill?"

I laughed as we ran off to my back yard, where I basked in

the sunshine of my friends' approval. For the first time in my life I felt like a hero.

My pals left half an hour later. As I entered the house through the back door, the phone was ringing. When Mom got off the line her eyes were flashing fury. The caller had been the incensed mother.

I was dragged by the ear to the woman's home.

"Apologize!" Mom demanded.

Head downcast, I mumbled that I was sorry—which wasn't true. The baby hadn't been hurt, I reasoned, so what was the big fuss about?

"This will never happen again," Mom told the unpacified woman. "I'm ashamed of my son. You can be sure he'll be punished."

Back at our house Mom grabbed an electric extension cord from a kitchen drawer, wrapped it around her hand, and paddled me. She was surprisingly strong, but the punishment didn't stop there.

When Dad returned from a revival the next day and heard the story, he was horrified. A hulking, tall, 265-pound, powerfully built man with a 40-inch waist, he unlooped his belt, pulled my trousers down, and whipped me severely while imploring Jesus, "Forgive him, forgive me."

Why was everybody uptight about an incident that had proved harmless? The breach between my parents and myself began to grow, and the double thrashing would not prove a deterrent in the future.

Being raised in a Pentecostal home was anything but a picnic. The lines between good and evil were clearly and strictly drawn by Dad. Everything "worldly"—unrelated to God—was off-limits. Smoking, drinking, and card playing, he sermonized, would pave our way to hell. Dancing was permissible only in church. If we listened to the radio, it had to be a religious program. Movies were forbidden fruit. If there had been television then, Dad wouldn't have allowed a set in the house. The smallest infraction of any of the strictures brought immediate retaliation.

19

My older sisters Donna and Faithe once borrowed a little makeup from a friend, and Dad strapped them for the innocent school-girl act of applying a bit of rouge and lipstick to their faces. He called it a sin.

Whatever I wanted to do was of the Devil, according to Dad. I became torn between his rugged standards and the far more relaxed family atmosphere enjoyed by all the other kids I knew. Except for smoking and drinking, they were allowed to do every-thing that was forbidden me. All the *don'ts* under which I was beginning to suffocate were taken for granted in their homes. Dad and I were headed for repeated collisions.

Loneliness became an early enemy. Mothers of my pals warned their children against playing with that troublesome Ruud kid—fallout from the unforgotten baby carriage incident. Donna, Dave, and Faithe rarely played with me—I was too young for them. Mom was preoccupied with running our home. With three other children, I couldn't command her exclusive devotion. Dad, forever visiting his necklace of churches in close-by Prince Albert, Meadow Lake, and Moosejaw, was a stranger. Some of his other churches were in communities so tiny that they had only a grain elevator—Saskatchewan was Canada's wheat belt—and a general store. He also preached in school auditoriums and at revivals in hired halls. But for all his evan-gelism, his collections barely matched our needs. Once, as I watched him hop into his car for another trip around his circuit, I said to Mom, "I wish I could die and go to heaven."

"You'll go there one day, dear," she answered, not realizing the loneliness I felt inside. My only reliable friends became my two-wheeler on which I explored the neighborhood and my mutt Ginger. I taught her a barrel of tricks, and she was especially adept at catching in her mouth the rubber ball I'd throw to her hour after hour. One day Ginger ran off. I heard later she'd been mashed to death under the wheels of an automobile. Why did Ginger split? I couldn't even keep a dog as a friend. I didn't get over her death for years.

I felt like a total outsider. I couldn't seem to communicate with anyone, and I began to develop feelings I couldn't share with anyone. No matter what others might think, I didn't consider myself all bad. Without telling Dad or Mom, I would kneel frequently beside my bed before going to sleep and pray to God for forgiveness, for understanding, for friends . . . for love. But alongside the prayers there were always the Devil's temptations, a superpower drawing me to sin.

Already I was a kid who instinctively did the opposite of what I was told to do. If Mom said not to crawl on the piano, when she came back into the front room after talking to a friend on the phone, my butt would be bouncing on the keys.

Next to the garage my brother, Dave, had a playhouse where he did a lot of woodwork and met with his friends. That was his private domain, and I wasn't allowed anywhere near it. Naturally, I'd sneak in whenever he wasn't around to look over his carved figures and inspect his tools. While I was in the playhouse one afternoon the adjoining garage somehow caught fire. The flames and smoke spread quickly. I heard Mom calling me, but I wouldn't come out. When the firemen arrived and doused the blaze, I was huddled on the floor trying to breathe through my shirt. It was a close call.

"See?" Dave said. "I told you we'd find Brian where he wasn't supposed to be."

The first person who showed me kindness I could measure and weigh was my first-grade teacher, Mrs. Dorothy Brown. A flower of a woman with red, bunched hair and cream-colored skin, she taught me to read and spent extra time with me after school helping me with my lessons. Never the world's best student, I needed and appreciated the additional tutoring.

Then when I was six Dad moved us to another house, a traumatic experience for me. My last day at Mount Pleasant School I bid good-bye to Mrs. Brown. "I want to tell you something," I said. "Please come real close." She bent her head like a curved rose to hear my whispered confidence.

I had nothing to say. I just kissed her.

At my new school, Wilson Elementary, I found my classmates ahead of me in every subject. I felt inferior, a failure when I couldn't cut it at the level of even the dumbest kid in the room.

Hard as I tried, I still flunked first grade. School was a bummer to me after that. I lost interest.

Early that semester, I feigned illness to avoid another embarrassing day of displaying my ignorance. Mom let me stay home. Left pretty much to myself, I wandered around the house and to my father's desk. I opened a drawer and found a treasure in one-dollar bills and change, about fifteen dollars, offerings from his churches.

Next day at school I played Santa Claus, buying every kid in class candy bars. My popularity zoomed, which was a neat feeling. It seemed to fill an emptiness inside me. The teacher telephoned Dad, as it turned out, telling him he was spoiling me by allowing me so much spending money.

When I arrived home, I was still walking on air because of the friendship I'd been able to buy at school. Dad was sitting on the stairway leading to the upstairs bedrooms. He looked at me coldly, checked my pockets, and found six dollars and fifty cents.

"Where did you get the money?"

I told him.

"I don't know what to do with you. You're not like your sisters and brother. Stabbing, stealing, disobeying your mother."

He tarred the daylights out of me again. It was bad enough that I had stolen, he said, but it was a double sin because I'd taken God's money.

All through my youth, of course, I was compelled to attend church and Sunday School, where I was an indolent, lackluster student. The Ten Commandments and the stories about those fossils in the Bible, from Abraham on, had nothing to do with me. In my groping, unsteady, insecure, and loveless world, the Bible was merely a fat book with small type, filled with fables, chockablock with back-to-back fairytales, irrelevant to a kid hooked on mischief and mayhem.

At age nine I ripped off my first tear, violating in one afternoon three of the long list of my father's *don'ts*. My triple play for Satan was composed of an introduction to smoking, drinking, and sex.

It happened on a Friday after school at the house of two kids I knew vaguely. Tommy Andreola and his sister Diane invited me home for a party. Their folks wouldn't be back until late that evening. I supposed they asked me because I had a reputation for trying anything once.

Tommy broke into his dad's liquor cabinet and poured some whiskey into an egg cup for me. We made a bar from an ironing board and pretended we were cowboys in a saloon. The drink scorched like lighter fluid. But the second and third drinks—and I don't know how many after that—went down easier. I choked on my first cigarette, but it didn't take long for me to get accustomed to smoking.

Soon we'd stripped off our clothes and were dancing nude throughout the house. Diane and I played at being married. We scooted into bed, fondling each other in tantalizing but unconsummated sex.

During the next three years I was in and out of minor trouble, always contrite afterwards. Life became a seesaw of right versus wrong. The best I could say for myself was that I had one foot rooted tentatively in heaven, the other firmly cemented in hell.

At age twelve, two significant events occurred that could have catapulted me permanently toward heaven, allowing me to bypass years of bruising grief and inner torture. Perhaps out of a feeling of guilt or a desire to do what was expected of me, I answered an altar call one Sunday morning in church. The visiting preacher asked me to pray and then announced that I was saved—I had come to Christ, accepted Him as Savior. A good, clean feeling swept over me. My folks were even cautiously optimistic about my future.

A few weeks later, Dad packed the whole family on a bus for the five-hundred-mile trip to Winnipeg in order to attend a revival.

We were sitting near the front. The evangelist had brown wavy hair and flashy clothes that I dug. Midway through his sermon, he stopped and pointed at me. "Son, come up here."

"Me?" I said with disbelief. I was terrified, afraid that every sin I'd committed was going to be exposed publicly.

"Yes, you with the long curly hair."

I rose, and before more than two thousand people he made a galvanizing declaration. All eyes were on us as his voice boomed

23

like an earthquake, the aftershocks echoing back to the epi-
center of the platform on which we were standing.

One day, he prophesied, *this young man is going to preach the
Gospel. He is going to be Canada's leading evangelist. He'll sing
the Word throughout America and the world and reach multitudes.*

He put his arm around me and I felt a superhigh like nothing
I'd known before. Then he had everyone bow their heads and
pray for me.

After the service, my folks were in rapture. "I always said
you'd be a preacher," Dad said happily, his eyes whirls of joy.
"Now it's been confirmed by God."

That evangelist, never having seen me before, had picked *me*
out of a throng and predicted *I* would become a famous sin-
buster. It was a mind-blowing experience. If there hadn't been
over two thousand witnesses present, I would have thought it all
a dream.

I'd heard Dad say scores of times that God worked in strange,
mysterious ways. But he'd also said that when God consumed
you, came to you as Master, He brought you to the summit of a
mountain. My reaction hadn't been quite that emotional or soaring when the preacher claimed I was saved, or when the evangelist predicted I was going to spend my life working for God. I
felt I had only climbed a foothill—but at least that was a start.

I began to think there must be something to religion after all.
I pledged to God that I'd never again steal or smoke or drink or
curse or play around with girls. Obviously, an oncoming evangelist who'd been handed an unexpected legacy of shaking the
world with the Gospel didn't do those things. Failure was behind
me, I thought, my sins forgiven and forgotten. Born again, I was
wildflower fresh, virgin pure.

After returning to Saskatoon, Mom sat me down and told me
about her first meeting with Dad and how they had both been
converted the same night. She said, now that I was also shackled
to Christ, that I was ready to hear about it.

Theodore Ruud and Valerie Olson were small town people,

24

born half a world apart in communities so anonymous they do not appear on most maps or in atlases.

Dad came from minuscule McKinney, North Dakota, The Flickertail State, which borders both Saskatchewan and Manitoba. His father was an alcoholic until he was saved shortly before his death at the age of eighty. Mom grew up on a farm in Naudstal, Norway, emigrating to the New World with her parents and celebrating her sixteenth birthday in mid-Atlantic during the crossing.

They met amid the golden arrows of a wheat farm outside Grande Prairie, in Western Alberta (population then: 1,724). Mom worked as a cook, part of her job conjuring black-iron skillets of bacon, ham, sausage, fresh country eggs, and a ton of hash-brown potatoes for the brawny, hungry migratory threshing crew. There was an immediate, mutual attraction between the broad-shouldered, sinewy-armed harvester with tar-black hair and the hazel-eyed, slim, blonde girl flitting like a gazelle through the big open-fireplace kitchen.

After the sheaves were gathered, Dad stayed behind laboring as an all-around hand. Their romance flourished for a year. They were married in 1936. Between them they earned seventy dollars a month plus room and board, a princely income for that Depression year. Hard times had sledgehammered Canada as severely as the States.

When Donna, the firstborn in our family, was five months old, Mom and Dad decided to attend a dance at the Grande Prairie Baptist Church, the only recreation available in the vast and lonely, thinly settled area. The ten-mile trip to town was hazardous and uncomfortable, the temperature thirty degrees below zero. There was no heater in Dad's old Ford, which bounced like a basketball, nearly skidding several times into the pyramids of snowbanks along the pitted single-lane dirt road.

Their heavy coats were little protection against the numbing, paralyzing cold. It took two hours for them to reach the church, nearly frozen, teeth chattering. The dance wasn't scheduled to start until a guest evangelist had preached, but they soon forgot about both the weather and the dance.

25

The evangelist was trying to storm the congregation on through to heaven, his voice loud and sonorous. The little sanctuary was a target for the booming cannonade of scriptural caveats he fired from his lungs, a hallelujah biblical broadside aimed directly at the unsaved.

" 'Get saved! Get saved!' He kept saying it over and over," Mom recalled. "I didn't know what he was talking about. What did 'getting saved' mean? Fascinating and dynamic as he was, I wasn't certain I'd enjoy being saved. But it was magnificent hearing him chase Satan back to hell.

"I'd listened to the Gospel often at our Lutheran church in Norway where they'd bring you right up to the door of heaven, then leave you just outside the entrance. They never taught you how to get inside the door, or so it seemed to me. This evangelist explained that unless you were born again, unless you reached out to Jesus as a child, with faith, you could not come to the throne of God, could not claim life everlasting. I'd never heard it put so simply and beautifully and appealingly. I decided I wanted to be saved."

When the articulate Satan-chaser issued an invitation to embrace Christ at the altar, Mom murmured to Dad, "Come on, let's go."

"Not me," he answered decisively. "You can if you want. I'm sitting right here."

Dad was either too proud or indifferent to heed the appeal. Mom was convinced, but nervous and frightened. She couldn't leave the bench to go forward by herself.

"If you won't go with me, I'll sit here too," she said with equal stubbornness.

They stayed for the dance, and during an intermission Mom told the pastor what had happened.

"The next time the Lord speaks to you, answer Him," the pastor advised, "no matter what anybody else says or does, even your husband."

The following night they were back, once more having braved the frigid obstacle course between the farm and the church. The evangelist was louder than the previous evening—rock-'em, sock-

26

'em, Bible-pounding, old-fashioned, uncompromising gut fundamentalism, hellfire and brimstone smoking from the pulpit.

Mom was fearful of a repeat performance. When the altar call was issued, she still couldn't bring herself to go it alone. She went slackjawed, however, when Dad rose without preliminary and answered the invitation.

"I was hurt that he hadn't shared the moment with me, miffed that he answered God first. But I quickly joined him at the altar. Ruffled feelings weren't going to keep me from Christ." Neither conversion ever wavered. Dad's, because it was so unexpected, was perhaps the more remarkable turnabout. He had seldom discussed religion with anyone, Mom included, and had shown no more than passing interest in God.

There were two immediate, important results of his walk to Christ: He gave up drinking and smoking. But though he was born again, he had not yet found his precise niche with God, was not yet the lion for the Lord that he would become. And he gave little indication of the deep and passionate faith which was slowly growing and building inside him.

In spite of its tranquility, life in Grande Prairie had disadvantages. Dad thought the ranch too isolated a place to raise a family. At this stage he also developed strong secular ambitions for success. It was time to move on. They went to Flin Flon on the Saskatchewan border in northwest Manitoba, a bustling town of less than seven thousand dominated by the Hudson Bay Mining and Smelting Co., Ltd. Dad began selling vacuum cleaners. He proved to be an excellent salesman, and began his rapid climb with Electro-Lux.

Aside from Dad's newfound career, the most important experience in Flin Flon was the discovery of a Pentecostal church. Mom remembered it vividly:

"We heard stories about the Holy Rollers, that they climbed the walls in the frenzy of their worship, walked on the ceiling, kicked down the benches, spoke in tongues. A cardinal tenet of their belief was to be filled with the euphoria of the Holy Ghost, the power of God moving inside you, to cry, sing, dance, and shout before the Lord with the fervor of David. We thought all

27

of it was the work of the Devil and we went only out of curiosity.

"I wasn't in that church ten minutes when I felt a stirring inside me. I could see immediately that many of the tales told about the so-called crazy Holy Rollers were nonsense, wildly exaggerated. The hymns were exciting chants of wonder, the preaching broke like waves over the congregation. Everyone was so happy in the Lord, praising His name repeatedly.

"Still I wasn't absolutely certain. I put God to a test. Feeling the Spirit overcoming me, I said to the Lord, 'If this is of you, I want to be filled by the Holy Ghost. But if this isn't godly, tell me to get out of this place and never come back.'

"I went to the altar and fell to my knees. The minister told me to raise my hands to heaven. No sooner were they outstretched and my voice lifted aloud in prayer than His power engulfed me. It was like a charge of electricity. It started in my fingertips and ignited through my entire frame. I'd never felt anything remotely similar to it; I had no idea the human body could be heir to such overwhelming, God-inspired dynamism.

"I was still so filled when I reached home that I couldn't talk intelligibly to our baby-sitter. I couldn't, for some reason, recall one word of English. I was speaking Norwegian, though I hadn't used the language in years. The baby-sitter must have thought me a babbling imbecile."

Dad was so impressed by Mom's encounter with God that he sought the same blood-racing, pulse-pounding Spirit. It took ten months—and then he too was filled.

Transferred to Saskatoon, he spent the ensuing years earning gobs of money. The year I was born he finally heard the call to preach and left his lucrative job, attended Bible school, and organized his Bible Deliverance Fellowship, an independent Pentecostal ministry. He'd found his niche with God.

So zealous did he become that in addition to his church-building and evangelizing, he put a sign on our front lawn declaring: *Jesus Saves*. Once he gathered thousands of signatures on a petition that demanded the government order the reading of the Bible in schools. It didn't become law, but that wasn't out of any lack of effort on Dad's part.

The recapitulation by Mom of her and Dad's experiences with God impressed me deeply. I was even more impressed that she had confided in me and shared so much, sorry only that Dad hadn't been there to add his reminiscences. I had never had a heart-to-heart talk with him. Now I understood why: Jesus was first, and laboring in the heavenly vineyard was a 24-hour-a-day job. Dad was deeply devoted to the Son of God. But didn't Jesus want Dad to be deeply devoted to his own son, as well? If not, something was wrong somewhere.

Dad didn't yet have a church in Saskatoon. The meetings he held in our home town took place at what was a booze and B-girl club when it wasn't rented to the Reverend Theodore Ruud for services. Dad wallowed in the challenge of fighting the Devil on his home ground.

Still inspired by the lofty prophecy of the evangelist in Winnipeg, I gave my testimony a few times before Dad's congregation. But I couldn't reach that mountain. I wasn't even making it up the foothills. Unaccountably, I began to tumble down fast. And I began to resent Christ because He was competing with me for my father's love, and He was winning hands down.

At the club one night a beefy teen-age friend of mine, Phil Carter, dared me to help him steal a wallet. Phil, his face still speckled by acne, was my equal as a backslider. We riffled a coat in the cloakroom, netting seven dollars from a wallet we lifted that belonged to one of Dad's worshippers.

I don't know how my father found out about it. But when he did, he was nonplussed, utterly uncomprehending, deeply disappointed that I had reverted to sin. Dad was forced to conclude reluctantly and sadly that the evangelist in Winnipeg had been a false prophet.

"I whipped you once for stealing God's money," he railed. "That was bad enough. Now you steal from the pockets of a man while he's in the holy, sacred act of worship. Only God can forgive such a crime, only He can redeem you. I can't."

I received the usual beating and the usual sermon, but my resentment bloated. Dad had misjudged me. He didn't understand the tugging allure Satan had for me. He was mistaken if he believed he could beat and preach me into religion.

29

I made one more effort to stay out of trouble. Physically lean and hard, by the time I was thirteen I had qualified for the school hockey team. The coach said I had enough promise to perhaps become a professional one day. But practice sessions and games collided with my forced attendance at church, and Dad ordered me to give up the sport I enjoyed so much. That further soured me.

I began to move with a set of new friends, all hellions—six or seven others besides Phil, interested only in raising Cain, tooling through town on screaming motorcycles, breaking into private homes and garages and scooping whatever we could.

I found I did have one useful talent—an affinity for flipping locks. Experimenting with every lock in our house, I soon developed the skill to open any steel fetter without a key. In my room I put together a modest but efficient burglar's kit—bobby pins, small knives, a screwdriver, and little picks I made out of wire.

That kit helped us to break and enter, and also helped me steal again at church, which Dad still insisted I attend. Before or after the service I'd slip the locks of the club's cabinets, taking whatever I could find—booze, cigarettes, occasionally small amounts of cash. The club never seemed to miss the loot, assuming that none of Dad's Holy Rollers were the thieves. Probably some of the club's employees were blamed or fired for my robberies.

The first outside caper that led to a run-in with the police came when Phil and I decided we wanted to give a party for our friends. We went to a supermarket and stashed steaks and cartons of cigarettes into our jackets. As we were leaving, we were collared by the manager.

The police were summoned. Phil, frightened, gave his real name and address. I lied and gave a phony name and an address not my own. Since our haul was retrieved and we were first-time juvenile offenders (the police had radioed headquarters and learned we didn't have records), we weren't busted.

The patrol car drove us home for whatever punishment our parents would mete out, stopping first at Phil's house. I'd noted that the car door could be opened from the outside only. The handles inside had been taken off. But from the outside, all you had to do was press the knob on the door handle. While the cops were escorting Phil up the walkway to his house, I rolled the window down, pushed the knob, and took off. "Stop in the name of the law!" the police shouted after me.

Whose law were they shouting about? Nobody's law but my own counted anymore.

I hid for several hours, and when I thought I was safe, I went home, congratulating myself that I'd outsmarted the law.

But the law had already visited Dad. Inadvertently, I'd given the police the address of friends who knew our family. "Nobody here fits that description," they agreed. "Sounds like the son of Reverend Theodore Ruud. They live at 927 7th Avenue North."

This time, Dad said, the whipping was because he loved me. I could easily forego that kind of love.

The punishment didn't end with a whipping, however. He careened me down the stairs to my room in the basement. I watched, horrified, as he took a long logging chain and ran it over a bolster of my bed and then around my right ankle. The chain had a padlock and he snapped it shut.

"I've preached and cried and prayed for your deliverance," he wailed. "Maybe you're not hopeless. Maybe by morning you'll repent and start traveling the way you should." A moment later, he disappeared up the stairs, walking heavily, leaving me tethered like a rogue elephant.

But Dad wasn't a very effective jailer. I took the bed apart to unhook one end of the chain, wrapped it around my waist, crawled out the window, and walked a mile in sub-zero cold. I broke into a locked garage and used a hacksaw to take off the chain. Then I headed downtown, swearing oaths at God and Jesus, profaning my father for his fanaticism.

The equivalent of an American birth certificate is officially known in Canada as "A Record of Registration of a Live Birth." Perhaps Dad thought it would have been best if St. Paul's Hospital had recorded the birth of a stillborn baby. The record thus far of this live birth was extremely unpromising in his eyes.

I hopped on a bus. I knew exactly where I was going. I'd

secretly violated Dad's rule against attending movies before, but a film had just hit town that I hungered to see.

As I entered the theater, my mind briefly rolled back to the image of Dad after he had finished chaining me. Before leaving he had cried like King David over his dead, rebellious manchild, Absalom, the fruit of his loins who had betrayed his trust. My name might as well have been Absalom.

"What have I done," Dad had asked, "to deserve a rebel against God and a gangster for a son?"

3

More Capone Than Christ

*He that seeketh mischief, it
shall come unto him.*

PROVERBS 11:27

*As a dog returneth to his
vomit, so a fool returneth to his
folly.*

PROVERBS 26:11

The film was a celluloid biography of Al Capone, a
roiling re-creation of the machinegun beer wars of the 1920s in
Chicago which, over scores of bullet-riddled bodies, brought
Scarface to power and world prominence.

I grooved on every bloody moment. The movie had a profound
effect on me, both consciously and subconsciously. Big Al,
smiling lethally under his snap-brimmed gray fedora, had proved
crime did pay. He lived like a king, with all the girls and booze
and high life he wanted. And people *respected* him. He had
more money and respect than my father, who was amening us
into poverty, who'd still be shouting hallelujah as they led him
through the door of the poorhouse.

33

I left the theater with delusions of grandeur. Could I become a mobster as big as Big Al? I could try. After all, I was on my way. My father had branded me a gangster, and the ambition had never quite been out of mind since I'd slashed that baby carriage with a knife.

Capone had had Big Chicago, and I had Little Chicago, which is what everyone called the West Side tenderloin of Saskatoon. Little Chicago isn't mentioned in the slick brochures of the Saskatoon Board of Trade and the Canadian Government Travel Bureau. They concentrate on the scenic wonders, the nearby trout streams and hunting areas, which because of my Dad's preoccupation with God, I had never seen. I'd never held a fishing line or duck rifle in my hands. Saskatoon, also known as the Queen of the North, has the natural and man-made splendor that justifies the name. The South Saskatchewan River threads through the heart of the city, lapping gently against high ground redolent with flowers, tall trees and broad streets. Added attractions are the university, an art gallery, and conservatory, none of which held any allure for me.

The town was founded as a temperance community by a colony of Methodists from Ontario who hated whiskey. They wanted a prairie Zion far from city evils. That didn't last long. Sin swept in quickly, including demon rum. Under Saskatoon's quaint, two-faced drinking laws, booze could be purchased only by those over twenty-one in government liquor stores, which closed at eleven P.M. No hard stuff was dispensed by the hotels and bars, only beer, though setups were provided by all these establishments and everybody looked the other way when bourbon or Scotch was poured from a flask inside a brown paper bag. Such restrictions gave rise to a flourishing bootleg trade.

"Saskatoon's early history, like that of most western Canadian communities, is sober to the point of dullness—entirely lacking the color and violence associated with the American frontier," writes Edward McCourt in his book *Saskatchewan* (St. Martin's Press, Inc., Macmillan & Co., Inc.). "No hard-eyed gunmen ever stalked one another along Second Avenue; no rustlers swung from the poplars lining the riverbank; the Mounties and the mis-

34

sionaries who preceded the settlers either jailed the bad men or converted them; church 'sociables' took the place of lynching parties; debating societies resolved disputes with words instead of bullets."

As I cascaded into young adulthood, nothing much had changed in Saskatoon. It was still dull. Boasting little more than a hundred thousand people, it was a modestly sized city with a small town flavor. News traveled fast and there were few secrets.

The economy of Saskatoon was based on farming, flour mills, grain elevators, creameries, and a sprinkling of light industry— foundries, machine shops, and tanneries. However respectable its facade, Saskatoon also had a respectable crime rate, one of the highest, percentage-wise, of any Canadian city. The causes mostly were boredom, the flatness of the quality of life, and the generations beginning to collide against each other as they were doing in Los Angeles, Chicago, and New York.

People were hard-working, and it was surprising how many of the hard-working natives and tourists ended up in Little Chicago where anything could be bought for a price. It festered with illegal gambling, bootleg joints, the haunts of pimps, prostitutes, and fences who'd buy stolen loot. It was a potpourri of small and not so small local hoods who were into everything that was outside the law, including a lucrative new commodity. Drugs had leapfrogged the unfortified border between Canada and the States, bringing with it new money, a new culture and life style. It was an entirely new and different scene for the flood of kids who embraced it, separating them from their parents, giving them individuality and distinction, their own thing in language, dress, music, clothes and morality. The bulls—an expression I'd picked up from the Capone film—were kept very busy. I was already part of that scene in every way, except for drugs. But that wouldn't be long in coming.

After the chaining incident, an uneasy truce developed between Dad and myself. I never quite forgave him for that. It ruined any hope for a relationship between us. I was a rogue, sure, but not a rogue elephant.

Besides vowing to give up religion and God forever, I spent as much time as possible away from home. I'd sleep in my father's house only as a last resort. Nobody in the family understood me and I didn't understand them. They had little choice but to let me go my own obstreperous, unmanageable way.

I hadn't yet made any important contacts in Little Chicago—I was hoping one day to join the biggest gang headquartered there —so I devoted myself to hit-and-miss capers throughout the city, on my own or with some of the like-minded friends I already knew.

I started shoplifting in department and hardware stores. I stole several hundred dollars' worth of toys and passed them out to kids in my neighborhood. (The movie had shown Capone distributing Christmas gifts to an orphanage.) I boosted a television set—the medium had reached us by now—from the waiting room of City Hospital and found a fence on the West Side. I became so adept as a thief that soon I could steal a radio and leave the music behind.

I not only stole haphazardly, but on order. I developed a network of "respectable" see-no-evil, ask-no-questions people who told me their specific needs—a clock radio, an electric appliance, jewelry . . . name it. Whatever it was, I'd scoop it for them. (I once heard my sisters mention they were short of stockings. I stole several dozen pair in their factory-fresh boxes from a warehouse. "A present," I told them.)

My two-way m.o. proved profitable. Selling directly to specific individuals brought fifty percent of the item's value, while fences usually paid only twenty-five percent.

I had borrowed my brother's car for most of my capers. Now I decided to build my own. I stole, scrounged from junkyards, and, when necessary, bought the parts I needed. I put that job together by myself—chassis, ten-horsepower Briggs and Stratton engine, tires, everything down to the last nut and bolt. Soon I had wheels that would travel up to sixty-five m.p.h. Racing one day alongside Dave, who was on his motorcycle, I failed to make a hairpin turn and I rolled over. There was nothing wrong with the car that couldn't be fixed and I came away unscathed except for minor lesions on my hands, which were in bandages for ten days. Crime and cars were action, speed, excitement. School, by contrast, was a drag.

Since the day Dad had said I could no longer play hockey in school, I devoted myself instead to playing hookey, taking off days at a time or cutting a class that didn't interest me. Often I'd split after lunch or during recess. I'd spend much of the time away from school driving up and down alleys, checking garages for tools, lawn mowers, furniture, electric trains, whatever could be scooped and sold. I'd drawn a careful, detailed map of the locations of the garages, and marked with a star the ones that had loot worth stealing. I'd return after dark and hit them.

Then I graduated to a custom-built '32 Ford, chopped and channelled, with a Thunderbird engine and three carburetors. I changed the transmission from standard to automatic. I paid for the car with my own ill-gotten money from my own bank account, but I'd stolen a couple of hot rod magazines and books from a drugstore which taught me how to make the modifications on the Ford. No point in spending when you could steal.

About this time my father began building a church on Windsor Street. He was welcome to it. I had discovered a new shrine to worship, one I could carry around in my pocket. At the age of fourteen I dropped my first pills—and to make it an especially memorable year, I was also expelled from school and busted for the first time.

I was running with a girl named Sally, and at a Friday night party in her home she started passing around what she called pain pills. I said I wasn't sick, I didn't need any medicine. But Sally persisted, "C'mon, we're all doing it."

I didn't want my friends to turn off to me, so I asked for twice as many as she'd taken, washing the four of them down with my sixth or seventh bottle of beer. For about twenty minutes there was no reaction. Then I found myself simultaneously drunk and stoned. I was laughing, sailing, in flight. Soon everything in the room became fuzzy.

I crept to a corner to enjoy my ride. I was coasting, rolling

37

downhill feet first. No hang-ups, no cares, no hassles. Not a problem under the sun.

Now my speech began to blur and I felt drowsy. It was a beautiful buzz, a smooth high. Man, I was having church, a kind of church my old man knew nothing about. I was having church with the Devil. Sally told me the pills were downers called, appropriately, red devils—Seconals

When I came down, I felt rotten. But Sally said that's the way it was—after the high came the low. The only surefire method for beating the low was to get high again.

I was on the psychedelic merry-go-round, though not heavy. It would take another year for me to get hooked. But when it came to sex, I turned on super-heavy, particularly with Kay, a 17-year-old girl in grade twelve at school, mother of an illegitimate child that she'd given up for adoption. Light brown hair and emerald eyes, to me she seemed a fully grown woman. Her figure was voluptuous enough and she knew everything there was to know about sex.

Our two-month affair came to an abrupt end one night. We were so spun out on downers that we got into my car for a ridiculous odyssey. We planned to drive to Mexico to get married. Less than ten miles down the highway the barbiturates lulled me to sleep at the wheel. We slid into a ditch. Neither of us injured, we stayed there for hours, first having sex, then dozing.

It was morning before we came down from our trips, both feeling miserable. In the stone cold glare of daylight, the coma of the drugs gone, we changed our minds about marriage. I maneuvered the car onto the road and we drove back, saying little to each other. After that, we went our separate ways, quickly drifting apart.

It didn't matter to me that I'd lost my favorite girl friend. For a teen-ager in Saskatoon, sex was as easy to find as a wheatfield outside town. It was as casual and promiscuous among young people spaced out on drugs as was adultery and fornication among adults tripped out on booze.

Having bragged freely to my classmates about being into drugs, sex, and crime, I was the talk of the school, wallowing in my notoriety. Whenever someone razzed me about being a preacher's kid, I used the opportunity to heap scorn on my old man and his obsolescent and outmoded religious hang-ups. My poor, misguided father—working at a frenzied pace for a religious freak named Jesus. Christ was outmoded, too. Church and Jesus, all garbage.

On what proved to be my last day in school, I was drinking beer on the lawn in front of the administration building and passing out downers that I'd scooped from a drugstore the night before.

I spotted the principal passing by on his way into the building. Though it was only the noon lunch hour, I was already high on a combination of beer and pills. I heaved my beer bottle at him, adding loud gratuitous curses. The bottle shattered at his feet, the shards of glass scattering like buckshot. Everybody stood silently waiting for the principal's reaction. But he angrily stalked inside, saying nothing.

When I reached my math class, the word was out that I was going to be expelled. I decided to expel the school before it expelled me. I gathered my books and announced to my teacher, "I can make it without school. It's time for me to blow this stinking scene." School was also garbage.

In the corridor I saw the principal and the football coach striding toward me. I guess the principal figured he needed muscle to throw me out bodily. He needn't have bothered. "Stick your damn school in your ear," I said on my way past them. I was an all-too-willing dropout. I'd been in grade nine, but had completed only grade eight.

I drove downtown and didn't realize I was exceeding the speed limit until I was pulled over by the bulls. After inspecting my car they confiscated it over my loud but useless protests, because it didn't have an emergency brake.

They left me stranded. I had no way to travel except to walk, and I wasn't in the mood for shanks' mare. I crossed the street to a movie theater and saw a shiny, brand new three-speed bike chained to a post in the parking lot. By this time I was so skillful that I could open any combination lock in five minutes. This bike was a snap. I flipped the lock and rode the bike home. A few days later I sold it at a fire-sale price of fifteen dollars to a kid I didn't know well.

That led to my first arrest.

The bike had been traced and the kid who'd bought it had finked on me. My folks blew their minds when the cops came to the house to bust me. Nevertheless, Dad put up my fifty-dollar bail.

I was charged with theft, violation of Sections 269 and 280 of the Canadian Criminal Code. Caught red-handed and with a witness ready to testify against me, I had no choice but to plead guilty. The judge read the charges, although I didn't pay much attention. It was just another sermon.

Smoldering with both rage and shame, Dad asked the judge for leniency. I wasn't ape for going to jail, and I was glad my father was speaking in my behalf. Let the Establishment con the Establishment. This was one of the few times my father had been useful to me. And it helped that he was a preacher. At least my old man's religious scam was good for something.

The judge sentenced me to a year—then suspended the jolt on my promise of good behavior.

I was too old and strong for Dad to beat or chain me anymore. So he gave me a tongue-lashing on the way home. His church had been completed and his congregation was growing. But he was getting a flood of personal complaints, letters, and phone calls from members of his congregation concerning my behavior.

"People ask me," he said, close to tears, "how I can preach the Gospel and yet raise a godless son. How do I answer them? You are destroying my work, destroying everything I value and hold sacred."

I didn't give a hoot in hell about his troubles. Yet I didn't quite have the nerve to use my favorite expression for anything I disapproved of, including Dad's Bible Deliverance Church. Face-to-face, I didn't quite have the nerve to call his scene *garbage*.

Though I'd beaten the rap and ransomed my car from the

40

police compound, there would hardly be a time in the next five years when I wouldn't have one charge or another hanging over my head, when I wouldn't be running from something or someone, running from my folks and family, from the bulls, from Little Chicago pals with whom I would tangle . . . from myself.

Out of school and with no desire to get a job, I swept into my fifteenth year on a tide of more thefts, pills, and sexual promiscuity. I was in a West Side bootlegger's joint one Sunday morning after gambling all night in the back room. I'd lost a couple of hundred dollars and was down from another trip. Cloud nine was so beautiful, but the trip back was a descent into an inferno. I had a booze and downer hangover, and felt like dying. Man, why did every trip have to end as a bummer? Why couldn't you stay high, high, high?

Phil Carter came into the legger's, took one look at me and handed me a blue and yellow tablet.

"It's speed," he said, assuring me. "Drop it and you'll be in heaven."

Virtually everyone I knew had tried speed, either in tabs, crystallized powder, or shooting up. They'd be crazy-wild strung out for days, paranoid, confused, violent.

"Man, I don't want to get in that heavy," I said.

"You're uptight, Brian. This is what you need."

Five minutes after swallowing the tab, I still felt like cemetery bait. I nearly retched, but willed myself into holding back because I didn't want to take a chance of losing the tab. In twenty minutes it was as if a giant hand had picked me up and dropped me into the middle of the ocean on a bed of lotus blossoms.

The run was starting. Phil was right. It was heaven. All the wretchedness, weariness, and dog-sick feelings were gone. The speed kept me on cloud nine until I went to bed that night.

Then came the crash, which was worse than ten hangovers. I slid and tossed on the bed like a decked fish. I fought imaginary monsters and tore at my skin. I flicked on the light, pulled the blankets off, and saw the most incredible sight of my life—my own heart struggling to burst through my rib cage. The peaceful ocean where I had been dropped had turned into a tempestuous maelstrom of anxiety.

I struggled to the phone. "Phil, I'm folding up. I'm on a bum trip, a real bummer."

He laughed. "Man, all you need is another tab."

I met him and he handed me one more blue and yellow trip into the heaven that would lead back to hell.

After two months of using Desbutals, dexies, whites, and hearts, I had a massive habit. And so I went into scooping heavier than ever in order to support myself as a speed freak.

I had learned quickly how to run the whole speed trip, from the initial high down to the amp out. Whenever I crashed, the only way I could resurrect myself was with more speed or for variation, downers or booze.

It was the speed that showed me something I never thought was part of my being. I would look at myself in the mirror and not recognize my reflection. I could look at myself impersonally, with fear and curiosity, wondering without knowing what a teen-ager named Brian Ruud, a stranger to himself, would do next. I was aware that now I was capable of anything. That was part of the speed-freak trip, and I accepted it.

It was always something of a problem finding a pad to turn on where there wouldn't be any interruptions or hassle from parents or the bulls. The perfect location presented itself when Dave rented a cottage near the railroad tracks, about five blocks from my folks' home. There were no other houses close by. I called it the Sugar Shack, naming it for a rock song that was then number one on the charts.

The Sugar Shack became the "in" place to space out, and I was always the host. Dave was around only in the daytime. He'd gone into the auto business, fixing up old cars and reselling them, using the garage of the cottage to store and work on his cars. I began spending more time there overnight than I did sleeping at my own home or the homes of my friends or in parked cars, the bus station, and doorways.

The pill parties at the Shack were frequent and notorious. A lot of dudes from Little Chicago straggled in to turn on. The cops heard about it, and not only patrolled outside, but frequently raided us. They never found any of our drugs, but picked up a number of dudes who were wanted on one charge or another.

The *pièce de résistance* party of them all took place one Saturday night. About a dozen guys and maybe twenty chicks took part in a bacchanal of drugs and intercourse. I took downers all that night and woke up early, stepping over sprawled bodies. I was heading toward the kitchen for breakfast when the front door opened. There stood the majestic figure of the Reverend Theodore Ruud. (He had come by, I found out afterwards, in another of his indefatigable attempts to get me to go to church.)

My father had preached countless sermons on hell and now he couldn't believe he was seeing it. Even I couldn't blame him.

The Shack looked like a cyclone had blown through. The glass picture frames Dave had hung were all cracked. There was a litter of empty cigarette packages, beer cans, and liquor bottles. Wall-to-wall bodies, wall-to-wall filth. Chicks half dressed, a few naked. Dudes spaced out against the walls, parts of which were smashed in. (I dimly recalled somebody pounding his fist into the walls to prove his strength.)

For once in his life, Dad was speechless. He looked at me with withering contempt (or was it pity?) then turned and silently walked away, his normally erect shoulders humped in defeat.

Feeling a pang of guilt, I called home later. Mom answered.

"Brian," she said, "how could you be part of something so disgraceful, so disgusting?"

Dad apparently had spared her none of the details.

"How's Dad taking it?"

"He's never missed a service since he became a preacher . . . except today. He's crying. Brian, you're crushing your father's soul."

Then the line went dead.

4

Cry Rape

> *The fearful, and unbelieving, and the abominable, and murderers, and whoremongers, and sorcerers, and idolaters, and all liars, shall have their part in the lake which burneth with fire and brimstone; which is the second death.*

REVELATION 21:8

That night I was restless. I should have aborted my speed trip with a couple of downers and gone to bed. The last place I should have split to was the West Side. But I was too fitful and fidgety to sleep. I barreled down to Little Chicago at twelve-thirty in the morning like a nail to a magnet, looking for action. I soon found more than I bargained for, a first-time scene for me. But there had to be a first time for everything—even rape.

I walked into one of the cafe hangouts where I could always find somebody I knew.

Cleft-chinned, red-haired Larry Davis, who had capered with me on a few occasions, was in a booth. Sitting with him was another dude I'd seen around, slinky, ferret-eyed, ghost-white. Everybody called him Spook. Ugly as a dung heap, he deserved the name. Also in the booth was a blonde, fairly attractive chick I'd never seen before, wearing a tight blouse and a clinging thigh-scraper of a skirt

Before I could sit down, Larry came up to me. "Let's buy some booze. This chick—her name's Anita—is a prostitute. Just turned two tricks in a motel. She wants to get loaded."

The four of us piled into my car. With Anita's bread, I went into the legger's and bought a case of beer.

"Everything's closed," Spook said. "Where can we go to drink the stuff?"

I wasn't in the mood for beer, but I agreed to chauffeur them because there wasn't anything else to do. I knew an appropriate spot—a gravel pit near the Sugar Shack. It was unpatrolled and out of the way.

When we parked, Anita turned the radio on, the rock sound rolling in with a clatter.

I changed my mind and started drinking. Half an hour later I was loaded. We were laughing and telling jokes. Everything was cool until Larry said, the booze lubricating his courage, "C'mon, Anita, give us a payoff."

"Why not?" she replied agreeably.

"It's your car, Brian, so you plow in first," Larry suggested.

Anita wasn't reluctant. "What's your pleasure?" she asked with a broad smile.

The scene now was a bummer. Who needed a gang splash? I'd dated dozens of beautiful chicks. I didn't need a prostitute, especially with two eager onlookers in the back seat. Besides, I was so loaded that sex didn't interest me.

"I'll pass," I said, and then for some reason I began to laugh so hard that I rolled against the door and fell out of the car to the ground. Picking myself up, I went into the back seat. Larry took my place in front. He kissed her for a while and then made out. After he finished, Spook took his turn. Because of my heavy beer intake, I barely knew what was happening. Larry and Spook urged me again to make it with Anita. I still refused. So Larry went back for seconds.

46

After that, Anita's mood changed. Combing her hair and adjusting her clothes, she said sullenly, "I'm just a cheap prostitute. I feel dirty."

I was sorry for her, and guessed that the booze had depressed her. She'd also mentioned that she was a doper, and whatever she was on was probably helping her downbeat mood. Maybe she'd dropped something before we left the cafe. None of us had any junk in the car.

"Kick her rear end out," Spook said.

God, he was a rat, I thought, his heart as ugly as his face. I was beginning to sober up and feeling conscience-stricken.

"Anita, how about some food?" I asked.

"No," she answered, "take me home."

"Home" was a low-slung, one-story pad not far from the West Side. There was a light burning in the house, and the minute I pulled the car to a halt, a swarthy and lantern-jawed dude rushed out, bellowing curses.

"Anita, where the hell you been? I had another trick lined up for you."

"This is Carl," Anita said. "My pimp."

"These guys pay you?" Carl asked, looking us over disapprovingly.

"Yes," she lied. I wondered how she'd square it with him when he found she wasn't telling the truth. For some reason I pitied the girl, which was unusual, since my sole concern was always for number one.

Anita trundled out of the car and Carl shoved her roughly ahead of him, again swearing at her.

Carl had hit me wrong. I disliked him. And not because he was a pimp, but because of the way he treated the chick who was supporting him. There wasn't any need for the rough stuff. I toyed with the idea of flattening him, but it wasn't my business. Pimps and their prostitutes were always battling. Why hassle myself over a chick who'd partied with us voluntarily?

I took off, dropping Larry and Spook. I slept at the Shack, and spent the next morning polishing my car. Then I went over to Larry's house.

"The police were just here and hauled him off," his mother

told me, worriedly. Her tone reminded me of my own mother. On the rare occasions when I saw Mom, she also talked in the same scared, bewildered, hopeless manner.

As I headed downtown, I tried to guess the reason for Larry's bust. Maybe for one of the capers we'd pulled together. Maybe the bulls were also looking for me.

I heard a sudden burst of sound: Sirens.

I was right. The heat *was* after me. From my rear-view mirror I could see two squad cars on my tail.

I decided not to make it easy for them. I floored the accelerator, getting as far as the City Hall parking lot where I made a U-turn on two wheels and whipped down the traffic-choked street. One of the cop cars managed to cut me off. I squealed to a stop. The bulls came over and one of them searched me. "No gun, no blade, no drugs," he said to his sidekick with obvious disappointment.

They took me to jail. I didn't know at the time that an all-points bulletin was out on me. I figured I'd broken a couple of traffic laws and that was it. I'd completely forgotten about Larry.

Instead of being questioned by the city cops, I was interrogated by an officer of the Royal Canadian Mounted Police. That was heavy. The Mounties only came in on big beefs.

The officer was in his fifties, low-key, smooth as oil, extremely polite. He wore a dark suit. The fancy red threads are for the movies, official government ceremonies, and parades for tourists.

"Mr. Ruud," he asked mildly, "where were you last night?"

The scene of the previous evening shot back to memory. But why was he asking me about that?

"Parked in my car."

"And where was your car parked?"

I had nothing to hide, so I answered honestly. "In a gravel pit near my brother's place."

"Now, Mr. Ruud, we have nothing against you." His voice was warm with reassurance. "We're certainly not accusing you of anything."

"Then why am I here?"

"You won't be detained long, Mr. Ruud." Calling a kid verging on sixteen "mister" seemed to be carrying politeness to the extreme.

"When can I leave?"

"Just a few more questions, Mr. Ruud. Do you know Anita McLear, Lawrence Davis, and Frank Zanni?"

"I met a chick named Anita last night and Larry is a friend of mine. I don't know the other guy."

"I believe he's sometimes referred to as 'Spook.' "

"I met him last night, too."

"Were these three individuals in your automobile from approximately one to four A.M. this morning?"

"What if they were?"

"Can you tell me exactly what occurred while you four young people were parked?"

No point in lying. He had the names and now I remembered that Larry was also in the can. But no crime I could think of had been committed.

"We had a little party, that's all."

"Did sexual intercourse occur?"

"Yes."

"Were the physical attentions of any or all of the three males in your automobile forced on Miss McLear?"

"No!"

"Are you certain?"

"Of course I'm certain. That chick's a professional hustler."

"Before you leave, Mr. Ruud, would you be kind enough to give us a statement concerning all the events that occurred in your automobile?"

"Sure, why not?"

A stenographer was called in. She was young, and I could see her blushing as I recounted the details of the party. When she left, I stood up.

"Just a moment, Mr. Ruud. I'm afraid we must detain you after all."

"Why? You said there weren't any charges against me."

"Mr. Ruud, there *are* charges. And the court will determine

49

your guilt or innocence. You are accused of violation of Section 136 of the Criminal Code."

"Which means?"

"Which means, Mr. Ruud . . . rape. Which also means, Mr. Ruud, whether or not you participated in the alleged rape, you are also charged as an accessory since the alleged rape occurred in your automobile."

I couldn't believe he was serious.

"Where'd you get this cock-and-bull story? That chick went along with everything. Check her out and you'll find she's a prostitute."

"That's beside the point. A prostitute can be a victim of a rape."

That struck me as a peculiar interpretation of law. I thought I was on a trip. This couldn't be happening.

"Who filed these charges?"

"Miss Anita McLear and a Mr. Carl Miller."

"You're taking the word of a whore and a pimp against mine."

Without answering he pressed a buzzer on his desk, and I was escorted to a cell. In the cells adjoining mine were Larry and Spook. All three of us were in on the same beef. We'd all had the same clever going-over with the same Mountie. I had to hand it to that bull. He'd sucked me in, played me for an idiot. Man, the Establishment could shove it.

I spent the night in jail. The next morning a guard handed me a copy of the *Star-Phoenix.*

In heavy type on the front page a headline read:

MINISTER'S SON ACCUSED OF RAPE

The story barely mentioned Larry and Spook. The reporter, of course, hadn't come around to hear our side of it, that we'd been framed. Now, even if I was proven innocent, the melodrama and flamboyance of that story would provide a long-lasting, juicy morsel for the table talk of Saskatoon's gossip mongers. Denial never quite expunged the original accusation from people's minds. Nor would a verdict of not guilty, which was a long shot anyway, since I was in a fixed race.

50

I wasn't a choir boy, but I wasn't a rapist either. I was a thief and a pillhead and a lot of other things. But rape was something else. It was the scummiest of crimes, and it appalled me. Even I had to draw the line somewhere.

The press could shove it, too.

What put the frosting on the cake of the whole weird predicament was that I'd felt sorry for Anita. It was a good lesson. The minute you let your guard down, the minute you stopped worrying about number one, you were in trouble.

From here on out, everyone could shove it.

Still I couldn't winnow from my mind a feeling of guilt concerning my folks. After languishing in jail several days on the bum rap, I tried something I hadn't done in a long while. I prayed. Not for myself, but for Mom and Dad, aware of the soul-searing one-two-three punch I'd hit them with: my arrest, the publicity, my jailing. I prayed that my parents' burden would be eased, but the clouds were brass and I knew I wasn't getting through.

My bail had been set at twenty-five hundred dollars, and when I called home, it was as I expected. Dad wouldn't talk to me. But Mom, sympathetic no matter what, finally prevailed on him to come to the phone. He agreed to see me.

Our meeting was taut at first. It was one thing for Dad to read about me being in jail, quite another for him to enter the corrosive atmosphere of gun-toting guards, bars, clanging gates, and other prisoners in the visitors' room, undoubtedly justifying themselves to their benumbed, shocked relatives, undoubtedly pleading they were in on a bum rap. That was SOP for all jailbirds.

"One of the most difficult things I've ever had to do," Dad told me through clenched teeth, "was stand before my congregation last Sunday and admit my son was charged with rape. I preached a sermon on rape. Since you aren't a student of the Bible, it might interest you to know that in biblical times rapists were punished by death. The Bible teaches that when a woman is raped, God is defiled. And the parents and the community share the offender's guilt."

"I didn't do it, Dad."

51

"You've lied so often, why should I believe you now? Why would the police arrest you if you were innocent?"

I had a momentary urge to bolt. I was already convicted in my father's eyes. But then, I couldn't blame him. He was right. I had lied habitually. There was no reason for him to take my word now.

The days in jail, with no drugs available though my body cried out for them, had made me extremely nervous, but had also induced a lucid honesty. I explained what had taken place in the car, omitting nothing. Dad questioned me closely. Finding no holes in my account, a sprinkle of relief peppered his still-concerned face. I had admitted to drunkenness, to being an eye-witness to particularly unholy fornication. Those were unthinkable sins to Dad. But he took what comfort he could from the fact that I hadn't touched the girl. He went my bail, and the next day I was back on the street. Larry and Spook had no one to raise their bail, and they remained in the lockup.

There was further irony looming ahead as the result of the scrape I was in: My trial was set for one day after my birthday. And I wasn't looking forward to the present I'd assuredly receive from the jury. Punishment for rape had been scaled down since the days of the Bible, but it still carried a sentence of up to ten years.

In a murderous rage, I scoured Saskatoon for Anita and Carl. But they'd crept into a hole somewhere, and I couldn't locate them. It was just as well. My towering anger, had I found them, probably would have ended in a double homicide.

Facing a ten-year sentence, I figured I didn't have too much more to lose. I became wilder than ever, mounting a one-man juggernaut of capering, racking up dozens of scores—garages, private homes, and especially the narcotics-laden shelves of drugstores. Always in the back of my mind was the dream of a big score. Robbing a bank was one possibility I considered. As was true of most addicts, I had also reached the point where I became a pusher. Since I was selling drugs I'd stolen, this brought a hundred percent profit.

The day of my birthday arrived—and I spent my last night of

52

freedom throwing a big blast at the Sugar Shack. Nobody sang "Happy Birthday, dear Brian." In an hour all the two dozen or so heads I'd invited were freaked out, and I'd taken so much speed I was wired right out of my skull.

"Let's grab some action," I said to three dudes helping me celebrate. "I'm going to jail tomorrow anyway. Another bust won't matter."

The four of us hit about a dozen homes in a new subdivision on the outskirts of town. Most of our swag came from liquor cabinets. It was amazing how much booze these square Johns drank. We had two suitcases of hard stuff, and in the car we chug-a-lugged whiskey, brandy, and vodka until we were hammered-out drunk.

I was aching for trouble, looking for a confrontation with the bulls, who were railroading me into ten long years in prison for something I didn't do. Why shouldn't I give them trouble?

I cruised down to Second Avenue, Saskatoon's main drag. Spotting a squad car, I pulled abreast of it and tossed a half-full bottle of booze against the windshield of the cop wagon.

"Try and get me, you SOB's!" I shouted.

Again the chase was on, but this time I wouldn't be caught. I hadn't forgotten the indignity of being outflanked in the previous pursuit. I prided myself on how skillfully I drove. I could have been a wheelman for Capone.

I gunned the motor, stamped my foot viciously on the gas pedal, accelerating to 120 m.p.h. Running every red light, I narrowly averted squashing an aged woman pedestrian and nearly banged into a semitrailer.

I turned onto Thirty-third Street and saw another squad car heading toward me to cut me off. I made a sharp cut into Seventh Avenue, and then jackknifed around another corner. Now I could count six or seven squad cars behind me, flashers whirling, sirens pealing. But I was leaving them in the dust. I swung onto Windsor Street, past my father's church.

On heavily traveled Spadina Crescent I almost lost control, barely righting the car to keep it from crashing through the guard rails into the river.

That was too much for the dudes riding with me. They begged me to stop long enough to let them out. Nothing doing. I was slamming the accelerator so hard, I thought my foot would plunge through the floorboard.

Reaching the highway, I could see a roadblock ahead. I slashed into an unprotected cutoff, powered on for a few more blocks and then careened into another street which proved to be a dead-end alley. The moment I braked to a stop, all four doors were flung open, everyone splitting toward a fence directly ahead of us.

One of the cop cars swerved into the alley, headlights tossing huge beams of illumination. I had one foot up the fence, and when I didn't obey the order to halt, the bulls began shooting, the bullets whistling past my head.

Letting out a blood-curdling moan, I fell to the ground. "I'm hit! I'm hit!"

"My God, we shot him, we shot a kid," I heard one of the cops say as they ran a flashlight along my doubled-up body. They ran to their radio to call for an ambulance.

I jumped to my feet. I'd been playing possum—the thing was all a big game to me—and while the backs of the bulls were turned I went for the fence again. I looked back and saw the rest of the squad cars arriving. As I disappeared from sight, the cops, realizing my deception, let go with another barrage of bullets.

Moving along dark streets until I found a taxi, I arrived at my folks' home, crawling through the window into my basement room. I hit the sack exhausted but pleased that I'd outwitted the bulls on what was perhaps the wildest joyride ever to burn up the staid streets of Saskatoon.

The farce of a trial began the next day at eleven-thirty in the morning. Anita and Carl—having emerged from their hole—testified against us, sticking to their rape story. When the prosecutor for the Crown finished presenting his "evidence," our attorney took over. I didn't think he was doing much of a job for us. He obviously felt our case was so weak he wouldn't let us take the stand in our own defense.

I looked at the jury, sizing them up as a covey of counterfeit

Christians. I was sure they'd convict us. Even if they didn't believe the rape story, they seemed the sort of straights who'd think sex among unmarried teen-agers was a disgrace. But I wondered about the members of the jury, wondered how many of them had had affairs before and while they were married.

Our attorney had found one good witness—a no-nonsense doctor—who testified he'd treated Anita after she'd taken an overdose of barbiturates six months before.

"Would you say Miss McLear is an addict?" our lawyer asked.

"Yes!" the doctor answered unequivocally.

"Is there anything else about Miss McLear's medical condition that would be germane to these proceedings?"

"She's under treatment for gonorrhea."

That still didn't prove much. Venereal disease was common in Saskatoon. An addict with the clap could still be a victim of rape by the curious standards of the law. What disappointed me was that our lawyer hadn't uncovered anyone who would testify that Anita was an out-and-out prostitute and Carl a pimp. I'd asked some West Side dudes and chicks who knew Carl why he was trying to nail us. I'd learned that Carl had terrorized Anita into joining him in signing the complaint because he was steaming mad at her, having discovered she hadn't charged us, and because he'd taken as much of an instant dislike to me as I had to him.

By one P.M. it was all over. The bulls took us back to our cells in the basement of the new courthouse where we sweated it out. At ten minutes before five the jury finally came in with a verdict, and we were taken back to the courtroom.

The judge motioned to the court clerk, who walked to the foreman of the jury and was handed a piece of paper. The verdict was read first by the judge. The expression on his face remained unchanged . . . no hint of whether or not we'd been found guilty.

I was between Larry and Spook in the prisoner's box when I heard a sob from the spectators' section. Glancing over my shoulder, I saw Mom. "Dear God, don't let my son go to jail," she prayed audibly.

The judge gave the clerk the verdict to read aloud.

"We the jury," he began in a thin, high-pitched voice, "find the defendants"—and he paused for a second that seemed a year long—"not guilty!"

Unbounded joy swept through me.

"The defendants, having been acquitted of all charges, are free to go," the judge said. "Court is adjourned."

I went to Mom. Dad was sitting beside her with his customary wrath of God mien. I wasn't sure if he was happy that I'd been acquitted. I was still a sinner to him and he said nothing to me. "Thanks," I told Mom perfunctorily, in my best con man style, giving her a fast kiss. "I know it's because of your prayer that I'm free."

Then Larry, Spook, and I fled the scene. We had a real excuse for a celebration. Now I wasn't even mad at Anita and Carl. We got juiced at the Shack. "We beat it! We beat it!" we boasted over and over, congratulating ourselves.

Later that day I was picked up again. The charge this time: dangerous driving. It stemmed from the chase during the previous night. Okay, I'd had myself a joyride, but didn't this town understand that I was reacting to the frame-up in the rape case? The jury's verdict proved the bulls had given me a bum trip. Now the bulls were persecuting me. Life was a lake of fire and brimstone, a gurgling whirlpool of a liquid monster reaching out with scabrous, scaly arms to drown me. The bulls wouldn't be happy until they had me behind bars.

5

Tigers on a Tear

*And with him they crucified
two thieves; the one on his right
hand, and the other on his left.*

MARK 15:27

*And one of the malefactors
which were hanged railed on
him, saying, If thou be Christ,
save thyself and us. But the other
answering rebuked him, saying,
Dost not thou fear God, seeing
thou art in the same condemna-
tion?*

LUKE 23:39–40

It proved unnecessary to push the panic button over
the dangerous driving bust—unnecessary if you were prepared to
gamble against the stupidity of the bulls and the courts, unnecessary if you were prepared to perjure yourself, unnecessary if you
were willing to pay witnesses to lie for you.

Without hesitation, I was willing to do all those things. I didn't want my driver's license lifted, or suffer even a worse penalty—jail perhaps. A lurid account of the hair-raising chase had appeared in the press, and more than four months later many in Saskatoon remembered it with glee or disgust, depending on who was doing the remembering. The West Side thought it a ball, the rest of the city believed it was the stunt of a maniac.

From the Crown's point of view, the case was open and shut. From my point of view, the outcome was definitely in doubt. In fact, I was sure I'd be found not guilty, so carefully had I figured my defense. It was as beautiful as it was easy. I felt so confident that I didn't think it necessary to hire a lawyer. For the first of many times, I acted as my own attorney during that preliminary hearing on November 6, 1964.

What I was planning was to some extent a calculated risk, but that didn't deter me from taking the chance. It would be a kick in the head to find out how smart the law was.

When the hearing got under way, the prosecution hinged its case on the fact that it was my car. The license plates and owner-ship papers had been traced. They had that and the testimony of the two bulls who both used the same phrase in identifying me as the driver: "To the best of my recollection, the vehicle was driven by the defendant."

On cross-examination, I extracted an admission from the bulls that their "recollection" might be wrong. Despite the head-light-flooded alley, were the beams from their squad car strong enough to outline me clearly? And in running the flashlight hastily over me, were they absolutely certain it was me? Could it not theoretically have been someone else? I thought the cops wavered enough in their replies to at least raise a doubt in the judge's mind.

Then I produced my star witness, one of the dudes who'd been in the car with me, Marty Scott. None of us, it had turned out, had been caught. Marty was a friend and a doper to whom I'd often given drugs—free. He had a build similar to mine and his hair was also blond.

Marty testified that he had borrowed my car and been at the

58

wheel during the chase. To nail it down further I produced two other witnesses, also doper friends, who swore that at the time of the chase I'd been with them in a West Side cafe.

The judge, an oval-faced dude with broken veins traveling along his puffy cheeks, snorted like a frustrated stallion. With utmost reluctance, he announced at the conclusion of the testimony, "The accused is acquitted."

I smiled and was about to split when the judge called, "Just a moment, Mr. Ruud." Then he poured out a scorching denunciation.

"If you have any notion that you outsmarted the law this time," he thundered, "or if you have any notion that by any great brilliance on your part in conducting your own defense in this case, that you have succeeded through those means of sustaining an acquittal for yourself, you had better speedily disabuse your mind of any such ideas." His eyes were still riveted on me as he continued: "There is nothing to your credit in anything that I have heard in this Court. It just so happens that under the particular circumstances attendant in this case, the Crown was unable to prove the essential ingredients of the offense."

I thought he'd never finish.

"I have my own ideas and very strong suspicions, very strong suspicions, as to your guilt. However, the case against you has not been proved."

Why was he telling me what I already knew?

"But you may find yourself in a situation similar to that of the pitcher going to the well too often. I would suggest that you see to it that you are not again in circumstances in this Court or any other Court under which the Crown has seen fit to charge you . . ." And then the warning: ". . . because your luck will not hold. That's all I have to say."

The hot water rebuke washed off me like the spray from a shower. The judge had blown his cool.

Beautiful.

I'd paid them back for the frame in the rape case, though this time I'd been guilty as sin.

The testimony of Marty and the other two heads had cost

me three hundred dollars, a bargain for the pride I felt in clobbering the law in its own ballpark. It was an especially exquisite sensation knowing that the judge and the bulls knew I was guilty, but couldn't lay a glove on me. I was altogether, feeling self-satisfied, smug, superneat.

From the courthouse I drove to my favorite West Side hangout, and there, standing in front near the curb, was the true Al Capone of Little Chicago.

His name was Alex Cordova. I'd seen him around and knew a great deal about him. Brown eyes, raven-black hair, he was in his thirties, but looked much younger. Five feet eight, tough and violent. If there was a stereotype for a gangster, Alex was it. He wore flashy threads, and was smooth and suave, a top-flight con man and into all the action in the Saskatoon underworld.

The bulls knew him, and even among the roughest of the hard cases on the West Side, his very name was feared. From what I'd heard he had Mafia connections and was personally acquainted with Joseph Zerilli, boss of the Detroit Family. But Alex would never make it big in La Cosa Nostra and was consigned to a comparatively minor outpost such as Saskatoon because he was a heavy doper. At the time, the Mafia frowned on narcotics to the point where some of the families wouldn't traffic in the stuff. But even among those families that did, the knowledge that one of their own was hooked was unthinkable. Being an addict made a man weak, an object of contempt—and worst of all, unreliable, unpredictable, untrustworthy.

So Alex had remained in Saskatoon, a big fish in a small pond, boss of all the bosses of whatever Mafia-connected activities there were.

Alex was my hero, though I'd never had the courage to speak to him. But now I was on a double high. I was up because of my acquittal and because the speed I'd dropped on the drive down was beginning to work. Swaggering over to him, I introduced myself, and confided, "Just beat the stupid bulls on two raps."

He flashed a grin and to my delight and surprise wrapped a strong, hairy arm around me. The smell of his cologne was overpowering. "You're Ruud," Alex said. "You've been pointed out to me. Always wanted to meet you. From what I hear, you're all right."

Up to that moment I'd figured Alex Cordova was out of my league, and I was flattered that he knew my name and apparently knew something of my reputation as a caperer. I was even more flattered at his friendliness when he invited me inside for a cup of coffee.

Alex howled with appreciative laughter as I recounted the details of the rape and dangerous driving beefs. He didn't say much about himself—Alex was well-known for keeping his lip buttoned—but he pulled out an envelope and showed me what must have been between five hundred and a thousand dollars in bills.

Since I was almost broke, the bread impressed me. I was never able to steal or push enough drugs to feed my habit. Every month I had to come up with several hundred dollars from scooping in order to buy my pills. I'd also had to put out for parts and repairs on my car and my all-around expenses, including the payoffs to my witnesses, had zoomed. Meantime, there was a lot of heat in the city. A special squad had been flown in from Vancouver, British Columbia, to crack down on narcotics. They'd successfully dried up some of the supply. There was still stuff available, but the price had nearly doubled.

"I could use some bread," I told Alex. "Anything shaking?"

"There's always something shaking—if you know where to look."

"Let's look together," I offered, doubtful if he'd team up with me.

"I don't need the money, but I'll show you a fast way to make some. I'll go along for laughs."

We got into his Lincoln and wheeled out to a suburban drugstore.

"See that little red box?" Alex asked.

I was disappointed. I'd expected important action from someone with Alex's experience and clout. The red box was only a stamp machine.

He must have been reading my mind. "Don't underestimate

61

it," Alex said. "I hit one last night and scored two hundred and eighty-five bucks in quarters. Not bad for two minutes work. That will give you gas and eating money with some left over to turn on. By the way, do you use the stuff?"

"Heavy."

The stamp machine was bolted to the wall outside the drugstore. No customers or traffic around. The proprietor was inside somewhere, out of sight.

Using my omnipresent baby gooseneck, it was a piece of cake opening the machine. I slid out the silver tray and emptied the quarters down my shirt.

Back in the car we counted over two hundred dollars. Not bad at all. "Keep it," Alex said. "It's only the beginning."

That night we hit another dozen or so stamp machines, emptying the nearly overflowing silver into a hat. It came to more than a thousand dollars.

After the last hit, Alex said, "You can stay at my place if you want."

I not only stayed—but moved in as a permanent guest. Sharing the pad of Saskatoon's prime hood made me feel a big man. His layout was cool. Alex's taste ran to black, white, and gold. Throughout the large, two-bedroom apartment, the furniture and deep shag carpeting were hued a rich salt and pepper. His coffee pot, dishes, and utensils were a molten brassy color that looked real enough to be gold. Alex was a dude who knew how to live.

My first night in his pad, we both turned on with speed. Alex was an ex-heroin user, who'd stopped mainlining only because smack made him so violently ill he couldn't function.

Up to a point, Alex and I became virtually inseparable. But there was a part of Alex's involvement in crime which he wouldn't share with me. He would ask me to leave the room often when phone calls came for him and he wanted to talk privately. He never introduced me to a number of well-dressed, older dudes who visited the apartment. I soon learned to split on these occasions without being asked.

The word on the West Side was that Alex had tentacles into

every racket in western and central Canada, including the manufacture and distribution of illegal booze, illicit gambling, pushing drugs, and organized prostitution. I hoped that in time he would bring me into these operations, especially if I impressed him as a loyal friend and a stellar thief.

Alex and I became a pair of tigers on a tear, hell-for-leather troublemakers. The crime jag on which we embarked was motivated only in part by money. Though he obviously didn't need the bread, Alex was game for any caper. Big or small, he grooved on the action as much as I did. Both of us were stoned continuously, which gave us extra bravado. Like racing car drivers fighting the odds against death, we were two daredevils running a race against the law, trying to see how long we could outlap the bulls.

Some of our hits were planned, some random rip-offs. Some were petty and not worth the risks we took. Some weren't petty but were executed with a precision that minimized the risks. It was only the action that counted. Alex had stated our anthem at our first meeting—"There's always something shaking, if you know where to look."

Following the rewarding assaults against the stamp machines, the next job was a downtown jewelry store. To case the joint, I strolled in, had a girl show me tray after tray of goodies. "It's got to be something special," I said. "It's a gift for my mother." I left undecided, saying I'd be back.

I *was* back—that night after closing, with Alex. The store didn't even have a burglar alarm system—their mistake. I sprung the backdoor lock, and we swept the glass display cases clean. I was only sorry I didn't have the know-how or the equipment to blow the safe. But it wasn't a bad haul—watches, zircons, and cultured pearls brought six hundred dollars in cash from our fence. Alex and I had agreed everything would be divided fifty-fifty.

The following day, about eleven-thirty P.M., we hit a gas station which had closed half an hour before. I jimmied a window, and we raided the register for what proved to be a scant sixty-seven dollars.

63

Eighty-three miles north-northeast of Saskatoon was Prince Albert. On the two-hour drive there we passed the forbidding walls of the prison. It was a small town of less than fifteen thousand people. We stopped at a hamburger joint and I checked the phone book for the addresses of local doctors. We broke into three doctors' offices, scooping all the drugs we could find and all the prescription pads we could find. There was a market for the pads among dopers, a hundred dollars apiece. That allowed them to take the chance of forging the doctor's name to get their stuff in a drugstore. Usually the druggist didn't bat an eye, even if he suspected the forgery. Like everybody else, those dudes were interested only in making a buck.

When we returned to the apartment, Alex's handsome German shepherd bounded toward us affectionately. Alex had named the dog Horse (for heroin) when he acquired him during his smack-using period.

Horse was hungry as a horse. Alex fed him a bowl of milk containing a blue stumbler, a downer marketed under the name of Amytal. At first, I thought that was cruel and unnecessary. I wouldn't have done that to my long-departed mutt, Ginger. But then again maybe I would—now. I was no longer a kid who believed a dog was a man's best friend. My best friend was Alex. Horse collapsed on the floor after the pill spaced him out and growled all night. A freaked-out German shepherd—wild.

By the next evening when Alex and I took him for a walk, Horse's trip was over. We passed a dark street and saw the open, lighted window of a two-story frame house. An old woman was asleep in a rocking chair, a magazine on her lap. Beside her was a large purse.

I picked up a bamboo rake and tip-toed to the window, effortlessly maneuvering the purse into my hands via the wooden pole. We went through it leisurely and heisted eighty-five dollars in bills, two blanks from her checkbook, and a letter with her signature at the bottom. A plan had formed quickly in my mind. With the rake, I returned the purse to the side of the still-sleeping woman.

On the way back to the apartment, I explained my idea to

Alex. He said it would be worth a try. He phoned a forger friend of his. "Baby, I've got a job for you. Get over here fast."

The paperhanger turned out to be a chick, and an altogether chick at that! Lorraine supplemented her income as a forger by turning $50-an-hour tricks. Movie-star beautiful, with floating black eyes and the figure of a Greek goddess, her calligraphy was as versatile as the sexual appetites she sated. Expertly, Lorraine duplicated the signature on the check. We made it out for fifteen hundred dollars, keeping the other blank check as insurance to use at another bank in case the first one didn't work.

In the morning Alex had his younger sister Angelina—about twenty years old, not as pretty as Lorraine, but still attractive—pay a visit to the woman's bank.

We'd crafted the scam carefully. Angelina was to say she was cashing the check for her aunt, who was too sick to appear in person. We knew the teller would phone to be sure the withdrawal was legitimate. Angelina was to give him the number of a pay phone. All went as planned. The phone rang at a cafe on the West Side. Lorraine answered, filtering her voice through a handkerchief. She sounded eighty years old, totally convincing. Man, that chick had unlimited talents. Angelina got the bread with no sweat.

We paid Lorraine and Angelina a hundred and fifty apiece for their help. That night we had a free-for-all, stoned-out blast, and Lorraine proved to me that her reputation for sexual versatility wasn't exaggerated.

Alex and I next turned to heel-and-toe capers. From a contact in Little Chicago we'd bought passkeys that fitted every hotel and motel room in the city. The best m.o. was to creep in late at night while the marks were asleep—or virtually anytime on weekends while they were sightseeing or in church. One Sunday alone we scooped maybe thirty rooms, snagging watches, jewelry, change, bills, anything of value.

With enough bread on hand for a while, Alex and I took a two-week vacation at Christmas time, turning on, partying, spending bread like we had our own money-making machine—which we did, as long as we could caper.

I'd phoned Mom once or twice, giving her the number at Alex's apartment. She called Christmas Eve to invite me to Dad's church services next morning. "It's the birthday of the Savior. Brian, you could come just this once—on this holiest of days." The hopelessness in her voice indicated she was merely going through the formalities of an invitation. She knew I wouldn't come. I told her I was busy and couldn't make it. Then I wished Mom a Merry Christmas and told her the wish extended to Dad, Dave, Donna, and Faithe.

By New Year's Eve, Alex and I were back on our tear, this time wandering into one of the biggest downtown hotels in Saskatoon. The entire lobby flowed with a Babel of drunken revelers. We sauntered around looking for a likely hit. In an alcove off the lobby were four showcases. The dummies inside wore Persian lamb coats and expensive clothes. Slipping the locks was child's play. We grabbed the fur coats and the cool threads, went out unmolested through a back door, leaving those dummies naked as Eve in the Garden of Eden. We stashed the goods in the trunk of Alex's car, then drove to a large motor inn where another party was in full swing. We arrived almost at the stroke of midnight. The lights in the large main dining room dimmed as the band struck up *Auld Lang Syne*. Everybody there was sloshed, too, and no one paid the slightest attention as we picked up a dozen or so ladies' handbags resting cozily and unwatched near their chairs. The juiced squares were still singing as we headed to our car in the parking lot. The music drifted into the Lincoln as we sped off with the loot that would bring us almost nine hundred dollars for the night's work.

"Happy New Year, Alex."

"Happy New Year, Brian."

But the new year didn't begin happily. The penetrating winds of Saskatoon and the biting winter cold all but form icicles in the air. Some days the temperatures slump to fifty degrees below zero. It was a job just to get the car started in the morning. Usually we had to call a tow truck to fire up the battery. The only heat in town now was generated by the bulls, who had carried out a series of heavy and effective raids in which almost every pusher in the city was busted. For the time being, even Alex

66

couldn't get any stuff through, despite his contacts. We had a small supply of speed on hand, but our cache of uppers and downers was disappearing quickly. Alex was talking about splitting to Detroit until the heat cooled. There he could get all the drugs he needed.

The crackdown was so tight it seemed as if the bulls had dropped an impenetrable curtain around the city. Dopers all over town were crashing down from their trips with no hope of fresh provisions. Like us, they were desperate.

I thought of a caper that appealed to Alex. We decided we'd hit up on green, heart-shaped Dexamyls, which could keep a user awake with no need to sleep for a week.

Entering a drugstore near the main drag on the tail of a howling coil of wind, I went to the newsstand, pretending to leaf through a magazine. The ferocious cold had kept everyone indoors. I was the only customer, which is exactly the way I'd figured it. It was almost three o'clock in the afternoon. At precisely three, Alex was due to call the pharmacist.

The phone shrilled precisely on schedule.

Identifying himself as a doctor, Alex was asking the pharmacist if he had a large supply of Dexamyls on hand. The roads into Saskatoon were so icy the trucks weren't getting through with his normal deliveries and his patients were running short, some already experiencing withdrawal symptoms. Could he help?

I watched the pharmacist leave the phone to inspect his shelves. He went to a large box in the middle of the fourth tier and looked inside. Cool. Now I had the exact location of the happy pills. By the time the pharmacist returned to the phone Alex had hung up and I'd disappeared into the glacial cold.

We pulled up at 12:45 that night. Alex stayed at the wheel of the car so we could sprint away fast. I pitched the concrete block in my hand through the plate glass window and ran inside for the scoop. I heard and saw simultaneously a rust-brown Doberman watchdog, which I hadn't spotted during my earlier visit. It was barking, leaping toward me, going for fresh meat. For a moment I froze.

I was no match for that monster. By the time I turned to head back to the car I heard sirens. The broken window had evidently triggered a silent alarm. Alex took off in panic as I watched with unbelieving horror.

I was stranded, but got myself swiftly together and raced behind the store into an alley. Fortunately the Doberman didn't follow, and the bulls didn't make the scene in time to nab me.

The night was refrigerator cold. I didn't have a dime for a bus or taxi.

The only lighted building was an establishment several blocks away that wasn't unfamiliar to me.

Bold as brass or stupid as a coot, I walked into the police station. No one was at the desk, so I went to the upstairs john, made a pillow out of paper towels and drifted off to sleep, the first I'd had in four days.

I was kicked awake in the morning by a bull who knew me. He was as startled as he was unfriendly. "Ruud, of all the creeps in town. What're you doing here?"

I explained I'd been caught last night without bus fare home.

"You'll be in a cell if you're not out of here in eight seconds," he said. "The station house isn't a hotel for bums like you."

"Thanks for the hospitality," I said, leaving without further discussion.

I hitched a ride to the West Side, borrowed a coin and called Alex. He picked me up thirty minutes later, full of apologies for leaving me to take the rap alone. "But I've got good news," he added. "One of my contacts made it into town with a suitcase of stuff—Desbutals, dexies, blue heavens, the works." Gratefully, I turned on with Alex and a vaguely remembered parade of chicks and dudes for several days.

Then Alex and I resumed our capering. On our way to hit two locations, a cop wagon on patrol pulled alongside us. They gave us a suspicious once-over, then left.

I was playing cat-and-mouse with the bulls, but I couldn't care less. It was a good thing they hadn't looked too closely at Alex. He was so tripped out that he was no help at all when I stopped at an appliance store and scooped three small portable TVs. From an auto supply store, I garnered a set of four new tires.

Spring brought a thaw not only in the weather but in the heat the bulls had been spreading. Everything loosened up, and everybody was back in action, doing his thing.

The hottest racket at the moment was stolen cars. I heard from the outfield—a code name for an operation run by a dude who specialized in the scam—that he was looking for an XL Fastback with bucket seats and a 390 engine. He and his crew specialized in remaking the hot cars overnight, burning off the serial numbers, repainting them, forging new ownership papers, and hustling them to waiting customers at a bargain price.

Alex and I cruised the city until we located a banana-yellow XL, the exact machine he would buy. Finding its door locked, I went to the trunk of Alex's car and took out my tools. I worked a screwdriver into the top of the window near the driver's seat, wedging enough of an opening so that I could drop a bent coathanger inside the car and spring the lock open.

I jumped inside and searched under the floor mats and in the glove compartment. Then in the ashtray I discovered what I was looking for—a spare set of keys. I drove the stolen wheels to the outfield, was paid $750, and met Alex back at the apartment.

We decided on another vacation, using the respite for one more journey into turned-on limbo.

No matter how much money I made from capering, it tumbled out as fast as it came in. When I was flush, I spent like a drunken sailor on shore leave. Pills. Chicks. Booze. Picking up the check for steaks at a restaurant for a dozen people. I'd never counted, but estimated I had thousands of dollars out to friends in loans I knew would never be repaid. I'd even insisted on paying part of the rent for Alex's expensive pad. That helped my pride—I wasn't a bum or a freeloader.

When I awoke in my usual fog one morning, there was a note from Alex on the table next to my bed. "See you in a couple of weeks." No further explanation as to why he'd split or where he was. A wave of self-pity drowned me. My best friend had let me down. I was disappointed and it was a blow to my ego. I'd come to depend on Alex's companionship more than I realized.

Broke and abandoned, I walked outside for a bracing shot of

cold air. I had to clear my mind. I had to think. The city greeted me like I was a leper—it loomed big and empty and lonely.

After walking for hours, I still felt low, confused, and remorseful. When I wasn't stoned or juiced or on a pulse-racing caper, there inevitably came the quiet moments when I had to face myself. And self-analysis was painful because it was always there, a feeling deeper than remorse—captured guilt. Whenever it surfaced the only cure was turning on, spacing out into a breathing zombie. As I walked I swallowed a dry tab of speed. Pretty soon the guilt would be gone and when it returned there would be another tab to drop.

I had no illusions about the life I was leading. But what other choice was there? Dad's romance with Christ? That was as much a bum trip as speed. Christ couldn't give me the high I craved. Go to work? About the only legitimate, negotiable talent I had was as a car mechanic. Assuming I could get such a job, who wanted eight dull hours five or six days a week of greasy fingernails for a chicken-feed paycheck?

I'd opted for the life I was living, chosen freely. But perhaps not. Maybe someone somewhere had rolled a pair of dice with my name on them. My point had come up snake eyes—and I was destined to be a perpetual loser.

The neighborhood seemed familiar. I found myself only a few blocks from my folks' home. I hadn't seen Mom or Dad since the day in court when I'd been cleared of the rape charge. How long ago was that?

Reaching the porch, the house looked different, not at all like the place where I'd grown up. It was as if I'd never seen it before. I'd felt at home at the legger's, dropping drugs, at parties, on capers, with Alex. As I opened the door I was a stranger to this house, a stranger to myself.

Dad was just coming down the stairs. His greeting was friendly and warm. He stared at me through red-rimmed, glassy eyes and took my arm.

"You're thin," he said, fending for words.

We both felt embarrassed, father and son with so much to

70

say to each other, yet with nothing to say. He ushered me into the front room. I still felt like a visitor in my own home.

"I'll get you something to eat." On his way to the kitchen, he called up to Mom. "Brian's home." My hands were trembling and my nerves tingling. The speed was beginning to run.

Mom came down and kissed me. She looked older. "Brian, have you come home to stay?"

"Just a visit."

Donna, Dave, and Faithe weren't around, and I was glad. I didn't want to face them, too.

"Stay, please stay. We know you've been running with Alex Cordova. We know what type of person he is, a drug addict and a thief. You're not like that."

"I stopped by to see how you and Dad were doing. I don't want to bother you. I'll be leaving soon."

She bit her bottom lip, struggling to hold back the tears. Then she prayed aloud. "Dear Jesus, this is not my son. But someday he will be my son again. Shine the light into my boy's life and heal him, bring him back to us."

The visit had been a mistake. Mom's prayer was bad enough, but when Dad came in with a sandwich, he added a sermon.

"I'm reminded," he preached, "of the two thieves who were crucified with Christ. One of them asked forgiveness, and Jesus told him while He was dying on the cross, 'Verily I say unto thee, Today shalt thou be with me in paradise.' Christ saved him and for his repentence gave him eternal life. Christ can save you, too. You only have to give yourself to Him."

I got up and walked past Mom and Dad. Saying nothing, I left the house and went back to my world.

I should have known. Home was prayers and preaching. Home was the same old, tired, unchanging religious garbage.

71

6

Wasted

The way of transgressors is hard.

PROVERBS 13:15

The wicked are like the troubled sea, when it cannot rest, whose waters cast up mire and dirt. There is no peace, saith my God, to the wicked.

ISAIAH 57:20–21

Still no word from Alex. Still a big, empty, lonely city. The only way to fill the void was with pick-up companionship on the West Side, although I had by now become somewhat disenchanted with the denizens of Little Chicago.

Now I realized the place was a jungle. I no longer harbored as gospel the two major clichés concerning life outside the law.

—*Honor among thieves.* Like me, everyone else was out for number one.

—*Crime paid.* Actually, it was a riptide sucking its practitioners under, leaving them bankrupt in spirit as well as pocket-book.

These were shocking discoveries for a seventeen-year-old with a long-standing ambition to emulate Capone. Yet he was still my only reliable hero. I still had to make it by his standards. At least that was what my twisted, spaced-out reasoning told me.

Jungle though it was, I had one advantage of being a card-carrying member of the West Side club. I knew everyone, everyone knew me. I had paid my dues to earn the grudging respect of my peers, who wouldn't hassle me so long as I didn't hassle them.

But this notion, too, was soon to be swept away. All that had gone before, all the weird and the wild of it, was to prove only a prelude to the weirdest, wildest, most terrifying weeks of my life, beginning one night as I emerged alone from the legger's, filled with my customary cocktail of speed and beer.

Three young dudes, who were new to me but looked as if they belonged in Little Chicago, were standing on the sidewalk. There was no preliminary as they tore into me, used me for a punching bag, threw me to the ground, jumped on me like my body was a trampoline, kicked me, then lifted and shoved me into a waiting Ford. My head slammed against the steel top of the car, and one final fist pummeled into my back, the last sensation I remembered before losing consciousness.

Even today, I can recall the ensuing nightmare only in flashes. Those longest days of my life come back as an incomplete mosaic. I'll probably never know for certain the explanation of the motiveless kidnapping. Most likely, it was a freaked-out doper's stunt. Logic is not an ingredient blended into drugs.

The time I was held a prisoner I remember only in bits and pieces, a crazy quilt of disconnected recollections. In that pit of darkness my mind ran out of sequence, jumbled tendrils of thoughts crawled through my memory—past, present, and future playing tag with my awareness, hallucination riding piggyback on reality, or vice versa.

I came to in the bathroom of an unfamiliar apartment, voices buzzing in the distance. Going to the sink to wash, I saw myself in the mirror, a fairly good facsimile of Dorian Gray

I must have been thirty-five pounds off my normal weight. My face was skeletal. Lumps rising from my jaw and cheeks as a result of the beating I'd taken. Left eye swollen shut. Dried blood coagulated around my nose and mouth. Hair matted. *Wasted!*

Food was a bar of chocolate a day and a bottle of pop. But someone was feeding me enough downers to keep me docile. Thank God for that much. Praise the Lord for creating the man who could create oblivion in a tab.

"I want to leave."
The response was a blow that went to my chin as a hammer to an anvil. I crawled to a corner and licked my wounds.

Charnel house de luxe, the scene rushing together· dudeschickspartiespillsboozenakedlegsspreadlegscurses.

Strip poker with a new twist! When a chick lost a hand she not only had to surrender an article of clothing, but a dude would press his thumb against her forehead with so much pressure that a goose egg was raised. A knife would circle the goose egg until blood began to trickle.

I was smoking a joint, feeling like a king sitting atop an orange crate throne.
Suddenly I was on fire. Hands pounding against me. The front of my sweater and shirt half burned away. Acrid smell. Lake of fire and brimstone closing in, getting nearer. Going under for the third time.

"Somebody, tell me why I'm here, pleasepleaseplease."
I didn't think I could take the kick in the groin and live.

What is that baby 1 nearly murdered doing this minute? It's old enough now to be a doper. Maybe one of the dopers in this

75

apartment . . . or maybe it's a bright young kid dreaming of becoming a nuclear physicist.

"Alex, where are you? Mom, where are you? Dad, send your Christ to deliver me."

Another chocolate bar, another bottle of pop. "Hey, man, don't forget my downers."

"How long have I been here?"
The skittering giggle of a chick. "How long do you think?" she says from a goose egg mouth outlined in blood in her forehead.

I can feel a dude grabbing at my head.
He yanks a handful of hair from my scalp.
It's literally raining hair—my hair—in the apartment.

Jut-jawed and dagger-eyed, Satan said: "Mr. Ruud, are you ready to make a pact with me?"
"What's the deal?"
"Deny the Christian faith. Deny the Creator of heaven and earth. Trample the cross. Believe only in me."
"I've done that all my life."
"Do you swear voluntarily and without coercion that your name is to be struck from the Book of Life and inscribed in the Book of Death?"
"If you get me out of here."
"Are you certain you want to leave?"
"Please, yes, oh God, I want to leave."
"You're confused. I'm not God."
"Yes, you are. Haven't I always worshipped you?"
"For the most part. But every once in a while you're filled with guilt. There's still love in you for your parents. There's still a part of you that's filled with God. You're not mine completely."
"Yesyesyes, I am."

76

"Are you absolutely certain you want to leave? This is paradise compared to where you're going."

"It couldn't be worse."

"Depends on your point of view. I can turn you on forever to drugs and sex, violence and drink. But there's a price for all those lovely, wonderful blessings."

"Like what?"

"My kingdom is as wide as it is long, an endless valley of lost souls suffering the anguish of the damned. Did you know there's a high bridge that connects heaven to hell, and from heaven's side of the bridge all those who lived for God, my everlasting enemy, can see the fiery furnace, the lake of fire, see my valley of the damned."

"I don't care."

"Think carefully. Do you really want to put your signature on a pact with me? Once you do, it's irrevocable."

"I asked my Dad to bring Christ and deliver me. Jesus didn't show. But you came, you cared enough to come."

"True . . . I came because I'm interested in your case. I want to deliver you."

"Promise?"

"As sure as my name is Satan and Devil and Abaddon and Apollyon and Beelzebub and Belial and Adversary and Dragon and Serpent and the Prince and Power of the Air. I'm called all those names in the Bible."

"When can I get out of here?"

"Soon."

"Will I get to meet Al Capone?"

"One of our most honored residents. An appointment can be arranged. Now sign here, in blood, of course."

I signed—gratefully.

Deliverance wouldn't be long in coming. I had it in writing from Satan himself.

The lights in the trip room are a fuzz of blue and red. People coming at me. Strong hands. Another beating. A rough one. *Why?* How long is this tunnel? Satan, you promised to deliver me.

If only they'd let me go home, I'd never fink. Which home?
1. Church and Christ on 7th Avenue with Mom and Dad?
2. The Sugar Shack? 3. Alex's yellow, purple, and blue apartment or was it black, white, and gold?

Some semblance of lucidity finally, inexplicably, was beginning to break through, an invisible needle puncturing the fever blister in my brain. The phantoms haunting me were gone, replaced by the passion to survive.

And the only way to survive was to escape.

A shower rejuvenated me. The aches and pains wracking my body were their own anodyne. It was surprising how much physical punishment I could sustain. I was weak, but not completely tapped out. Taking full advantage of the fresh spurt of energy, I made my first, short-lived attempt to free myself.

Above the sink in the john were two windows. I slid them back after unscrewing the screens. The procedure emitted a telling squeal of noise that was overheard. My captors jiggled the lock on the door. When I refused to open it, they broke it down.

"You trying to leave us?" said one of the dudes, bearded, chunky, jackal-mean. "Haven't you been enjoying our hospitality?" There was a dull piece of wood in his hand. All at once, like the rod of Moses turned serpent, the wood transformed itself into a switchblade.

He came toward me. I managed to sidestep his first lunge, though I was nicked in the arm.

"Finish him off," someone called.

Using my feet and arms in an ungraceful pirouette, I kept dancing away from him for several moments.

Then they tired of the rat-in-the-corner game. "He's kind of cute," said the girl with the skittering laugh. "Leave him alone."

"What are we going to do with him?" It was the voice of the girl who'd saved me from being cut. "He's been here six weeks."

"I'll think of something," said the dude with the switchblade. "One thing for sure—he'll never get out alive."

At that precise instant, another dude burst into the apartment.

78

"Fuzz!" he shouted. "I heard the sirens downstairs. They busted Frank this morning. He must have told them where we are."

The dozen or so bodies in the room came to life and flung themselves through the door, forgetting me completely, leaving me alone in the apartment. I was free—almost.

I wasn't anxious for the bulls to find me there. They would shortly be raiding the place for some reason. Whatever it was, I didn't want the beef pinned on me. I ran out the door and down to the basement, finding a hiding place between the boiler and the wall.

I could hear clumping, ponderous footsteps above me and then the basement door opened, a flashlight touring the dank, dark underbelly of the building. "Nobody's here," a bull's voice said.

Finally, they left. The prisoner who nobody knew was a prisoner was—at last—no longer a prisoner. Satan had kept his word—he'd delivered me.

Growing up in a cold climate, the body becomes a thermometer. Mine told me it was at least twenty-five degrees below zero as I hit the street, walking as briskly as I could, headed for Phil Carter's pad. I needed quick help from someone. Phil and I had known each other since we were kids. We'd scooped together many times. Next to Alex, I considered him my closest friend.

Phil had left home to live by himself. Last I'd heard his bread came from a part-time job as a short-order cook and occasional capers. Moving by his neat, wire-wheeled Sunbeam, a car he'd bought with money from some of our old capers, I knocked on his door. It was a long time until my pounding was heard above the flare of high-pitched voices and blaring music inside.

"Where you been, Brian?" Phil asked casually. "We all thought you blew town."

"Man, I need some food, a place to stay, a few bucks. Help me."

A group of dudes and chicks swept up behind Phil. I knew every one of them, but that wasn't about to win me any points.

The rebukes stung like wasp bites: "The great Brian Ruud. He doesn't look like much to me."

"Looks like a freak."

"Phil, kick that miserable bastard out of here."

"Sorry, Brian," Phil said, slamming the door in my face.

So much for honor among thieves. My thermometer said it was even colder when I slumped out to the street again.

Still wearing my half-burned sweater as a useless shield against the spears of winter, I went to the only place left to go.

Retrieving the key from the hidden nail above my folks' front door, I let myself in and—famished—went immediately to the kitchen. I grabbed a piece of charred toast and was opening the refrigerator when I heard footsteps.

Good God, it was great to see my brother, Dave.

"What the hell are you doing here?" His voice was lash and fury. "Get out! Go back to your thug friends. You only come home to freeload. You only come home to steal from us and bring more trouble and pain to Mom and Dad."

Then he grabbed me and threw me against the wall. My last ounce of strength was gone and I was helpless as he started throwing punches at me.

I couldn't blame Dave. Everything he'd said was true. But if he tossed me out I knew I'd crumple up and die in the freezing winter air.

"Stop it!" The command was from Dad. "Dave, leave him alone. Can't you see he's sick and needs help?" How long had it been since I'd met a Good Samaritan? How long since anyone had shown kindness and compassion?

I slept for three solid days, waking only to eat. Then I went back to sleep, for twelve and eighteen hours at a clip.

At the end of two weeks, I was beginning to heal. Had that six-week nightmare really happened?

I sloughed it off. Anger and revenge were pointless. Besides, I had other fish to fry. Those dopers had had their kicks. And I was myself perfectly capable of pulling the same stunt on some other hapless pillhead. I had no interest in finding my captors. What good would it do if I did? I hadn't told the story to anyone. Who'd believe me? If I complained to the bulls, they'd say I'd gotten only half of what I deserved.

As my strength came back, so did my confidence. After recuperating for about a month, I was together, feeling fit and ready for my next move. I left the house on Sunday morning, about nine-thirty, while the family was in church. I left the house with almost fifty dollars scooped from Dad's desk drawer, thinking Good Samaritans were sheep, put on earth to be fleeced.

7

From Thy Wounded Side

*Whoso despiseth the word
shall be destroyed.*

PROVERBS 13:13

*If thine eye be evil, thy whole
body shall be full of darkness.*

MATTHEW 6:23

Less than a week later, I was in jail.

After leaving my folks' house I went directly to Alex's pad, thinking I could at least look in on Horse. I didn't know whether or not the dog was being fed while Alex was gone. Maybe I could take Horse for a walk.

As I let myself in with my key, both Horse and Alex came to greet me. Alex and I threw our arms around each other like reunited brothers. It was a happy reunion. Since Alex didn't volunteer an explanation concerning his absence, I knew it would be unwise to pry. I didn't tell him about the time I'd had during my kidnapping. The past was frozen, unchangeable.

What mattered was today, now. Whenever possible, I avoided making plans more than twenty-four hours in advance. There was more surprise and excitement to life that way.

Alex gave me six Dezies and we both turned on.

What was shaking now, we decided, was another motel, a cinch hit. This time, instead of scooping individual rooms, we'd go for the storage room of a large motel, which is usually as swollen with goodies as a piñata.

It was simple to gain entrance with my baby gooseneck crowbar. To avoid fingerprint detection, I'd added one more item to my burglar's kit—a pair of tight, pink rubber physician's gloves. I wanted no slipup.

The storeroom yielded a modest bonanza—two cases of wine, electric guitars, portable radios, shavers, and cool threads. We piled the stash into the back seat and trunk of the car.

Although we'd planned the caper with caution, I nevertheless made two mistakes: driving my own car and losing my cool. As we pulled out of the motel's parking lot, a cop wagon was pulling in. I panicked, wheeling off fast—but not, I would soon learn, fast enough.

Our loot brought $110, a disappointing net, and so I began planning our biggest caper yet, an armed robbery that might bring as much as ten thousand dollars in cash, probably more.

That caper had to be postponed, however. I was arrested three days after the motel job, charged with theft and breaking and entering. A sharp-eyed bull in the cop wagon had noted the make of my car and the license number.

Appearing as my own attorney proved I was no F. Lee Bailey. It seemed I had a fool for a client. The prosecutor had me cold. (I hadn't implicated Alex, proving to my own satisfaction that I was one thief with some semblance of honor.)

The judge, fortunately, was not the same one who'd scourged and warned me in the dangerous driving case. He sentenced me to thirty days in Prince Albert. He said he was being "lenient" because of my youth and due to the fact that the two bulls couldn't positively identify me as being at the wheel of the car. I'd forced that admission from them during my cross-examination. The prosecutor, veins nearly bursting from his neck, told the judge I was a "habitual criminal" and deserved a more severe sentence.

Everything considered, maybe F. Lee Bailey couldn't have handled my defense better.

Wearily, Mom and Dad visited me in prison. So did Donna and her new husband, an all-right dude named Dr. Douglas George Roberts, who was now an intern and who in a few years would become one of the outstanding physicians in Victoria, British Columbia.

A psychiatrist gave me the once-over. The task force lectured and sermonized. I'd never had any shortage of pious advice and preaching. Too damn much of it, in fact.

Promising that I would mend my ways was another con job, but the visit proved worthwhile in one respect. Mom brought some extra food and Dad gave me a little money. The home-cooked turkey and cake were a welcome relief to the slop served in the slammer. I used the money to buy cigarettes, pot, and whatever type of uppers and downers could be smuggled into the prison. There was a lively trade in drugs behind the walls.

I found prison anything but glamorous. The days were spent in a dull drag of sorting potatoes and mopping floors. When my sentence was over, I was handed a bus ticket and a lecture by the warden that added up to the injunction to go and sin no more.

But sin was waiting for me outside the prison gate in the person of Alex and two of his friends. I climbed into the car and somebody shoved a tab and a bottle of beer into my hands. Soon we were all loaded, as was the Lincoln—with a small armory of rifles and pistols.

The four of us took off on an ad-lib eight-week robbery jag, sticking up a fried chicken joint, scooping doctors' offices, writing our own prescriptions on stolen blanks. We also broke into dozens of drugstores, service stations, and jewelry stores. By now I was an expert, holding a high-powered rifle just in case. My job during most of these hits was tripping the locks.

"Anybody who even smells suspicious, blow his head off," was Alex's order.

No one happened to interfere with us while we were in the process of scores of robberies, which was both miraculous and fortunate. I was prepared to gun down anybody who might spoil our action. Alex by this time had developed a hypnotic power over me, and not me alone. He could literally look at a chick who was a virgin and transform her overnight into a prostitute. He could take a freckle-faced schoolboy of thirteen and make a head out of him in short order. Sometimes when I looked at Alex, I thought I was seeing Satan, so much did he resemble the Devil with whom I'd signed a pact during my strung-out reverie in the dopers' hideout.

Our spree carried us all the way to Winnipeg and back. When we rolled into Saskatoon on a Sunday night, on impulse I asked Alex to drop me at Dad's church. He would be holding his evening service. I hadn't seen my folks since leaving prison, and they didn't know if I was alive or dead. It wouldn't hurt to put in an appearance. Might even be a ball if Dad was denouncing me again from his pulpit. Standing on the sidewalk I had one pocket brimming with pills, the other with hundred-dollar bills. The felonious foray had been extremely successful.

Wafting out from the building were the strains of a hymn I'd heard since I was a kid.

> Rock of ages, cleft for me,
> Let me hide myself in Thee:
> Let the water and the blood,
> From Thy wounded side which
> flowed . . .

I wouldn't know until later how prophetic that last line would be, that I would suffer a similar body cut to the one attributed to Christ.

I sat down in the last row of pews as the congregation continued singing.

> Be of sin the double cure,
> Save from wrath and make me
> pure,
> Rock of Ages, cleft for me,
> Let me hide myself in Thee.

I was already bored. The church was full and here were all these hypocrites babbling a hymn nearly two hundred years old and supposedly living by the principles of a Book thousands of years old. What did all that hoary stuff have to do with me or with the way life was being led in 1965? What sort of trip was that? Grooving on a mess of ancient mumbo-jumbo

Heads turned and dissected me like I was a wriggling bug under a microscope. "Gangster," "addict," "pusher," "jailbird," "preacher's son gone wrong," they were thinking. I wondered how much microscopic inspection *their* lives could stand.

I heard my name called from the pulpit. "Brian, it's so good to see you. Bless you, my son."

Dad didn't have sense enough to ignore me. Why should he call attention to his prodigal who stood foursquare in opposition to everything he believed?

Dad made a few announcements and then introduced a visiting soul-saver from the States. He was Reverend Don Kennedy, a young dude no more than thirty, who wore a smug, self-righteous expression under his halo of brown hair. I read him as just another religious scam artist who no doubt was wondering how fat the offering would be. Everybody had a racket.

The sermon began and from its content I knew that Reverend Kennedy was losing no time in libeling me. From the bow of his mouth came the arrows of unsubtle homilies, his quiver filled with references to all the young dudes in the Bible who'd fouled up. Absalom sounded super-cool, a biblical hippie. He'd been antiestablishment and worn his hair long. While he was splitting from his father's army on horseback, his hair got caught in the branches of a tree. He hung there helplessly until some old general named Joab came up and finished him off, hurling three javelins into his body. Then Reverend Kennedy talked about Adonijah, who was killed by his brother, King Solomon, in a freaky battle for the throne of Israel. Rehoboam, Solomon's son, was another big disappointment to his father. And somebody named Jeroboam had put out a contract to hit Solomon until that crafty old codger put out a contract on Jeroboam, forcing him into exile in Egypt. All those dudes ended up dead or in big trouble. It was amazing how many young dudes had fouled up in my old man's favorite Book. But by now I was tiring of it. So what?

The tedium of the sin-belter's uncamouflaged message to me became too much. From my shirt pocket I extracted a handful of sunflower seeds. When I was through munching them, loudly as possible, I reached for a songbook and spit the shells between the pages.

Midway through the sermon I got up and went downstairs to the john. When I couldn't find a drinking glass, I dropped a couple of tabs, cupping my hands under the tap to wash them down. Chuckling, I went back to the service.

By the time the sermon concluded I was coasting. As the congregation stood for the final prayer, I walked outside, looking back when I heard my name called.

"Brian," Reverend Kennedy said, "why not get right with the Lord?"

Another fanatic. Did this con man think he could suddenly pump religion into me when all my life Dad and others had failed? Maybe Dad had offered him an extra couple of bucks if he could save me.

"Split, man," I said.

He ran after me and grabbed my arm, spinning me around. His face, taut with fervor, was an inch from mine. "If you don't get right with God now, you're going to wish you had. If you don't get right, something dreadful is going to happen to you in the next few days."

I shucked off his grip and pushed him away. My parry to his thrust included an old, comfortable phrase, "I don't need your garbage religion. You have your trip, I have mine. Let's keep it that way."

As I took off his last words rang in my ears. "The Devil's going to get you."

A lot he knew. I could curl the pages of his Bible if I told him about the working arrangement I already had with the Devil. I went to Alex's pad and found a party going full blast.

"Hey, Brian," Alex said, "how was church?"

"Wild. A preacher told me that if I don't get right with God, the Devil's going to get me. He said something terrible is going to happen to me."

After everyone stopped screaming with laughter, Alex winked knowingly at me. The wink indicated a secret shared only by Alex and myself.

I spent most of my time the next Monday, Tuesday, Wednesday, and Thursday minutely casing the big job Alex and I had planned before my jolt in Prince Albert. We were going to pull it off by ourselves. Friday was payday at the largest creamery in town, and there had to be a minimum of ten grand stashed in the two safes. We planned the hit for early Friday morning before anyone arrived for work.

I had checked, double-checked, and rechecked every detail. The car we were going to use was filled with gas, was in perfect working order, and was souped up so that we could outdistance any pursuers.

It was a little past midnight on Friday morning as I made the final check and the last preparations.

I drove across town and parked two blocks from the creamery. I walked the rest of the way through a long alley and went to a ground-floor window near a loading dock that was hidden by a clump of bushes. Gingerly, I disconnected the burglar alarm system and left the window slightly ajar.

Then I ran across the street and climbed the roof of a garage. I lit a cigarette and waited.

Right on schedule, at five minutes to one, a bull appeared to make his rounds. He danced his flashlight across the doors and windows of the building, but missed the tampered window. Satisfied, he went back to his patrol car, joined his buddy, and they took off.

There wouldn't be another check on this beat for exactly four hours. By that time Alex and I would have money to burn. As a final precaution, we both planned to pack guns on this caper in case something went wrong. If someone stumbled onto us unexpectedly, more likely than not that luckless dude would end up dead.

Everything was in readiness, including the safe-cracking paraphernalia in the trunk of the car that I was certain would open the steel boxes. Now I was on my way to pick up Alex.

To establish an alibi, Alex and I had arranged to have a party that night. Fifteen or so dopers were invited. If all went as expected—if we weren't spotted in the act of scooping the safes, if we weren't chased by the bulls—our plan was to return to the blast immediately following the caper. Everyone there would swear we'd never left the premises. The alibi would be foolproof.

Alex's pad was on the second floor of a three-story building. As I opened the downstairs entrance door and took the steps three at a time, I heard a gunshot. The building shook like an aspen caught in a cyclone. Sounded like too much party, much too much.

The first thing I saw when I entered the pad was a freak at the far end of the living room holding a rifle. He let go with another shot and everybody ducked for cover. The slug crashed into a stack of LP's, scattering the pieces like confetti.

I was furious. "What the hell is going on?" I shouted at Alex. "Do you want every bull in town down on us?"

Instead of replying, Alex and five other dudes picked themselves up from the floor and came toward me. Something was wrong. The air crackled with tension. I didn't at all care for the unfriendly looks on the faces of Alex and the others who now had me surrounded. Alex was calmly indulging in his favorite pastime—shaving Canadian-made bullets, whittling them down to fit his small American handgun.

In a moment it became apparent why I was being hemmed in, why I was the center of attention. Alex, uncharacteristically, had spilled the details of the job, drugs no doubt loosening his tongue.

The dudes made no secret of what was bugging them. Suddenly, all my buddies had reasons for hating me. Several flat-out resented that they weren't going to be cut in on the profitable creamery caper. Another accused me of pirating his chick. Most unexpected of all, Alex said I'd been holding out loot and drugs from some of our previous capers. The room was a pressure cooker—heavy with menace, violence on a chain tugging to run free.

90

I was about to plead with Alex to call off the goons—maybe this was just a practical joke. I never got the chance.

Without realizing it was heading toward me, I saw a butcher knife arc through the air. Then the floor came up, the ceiling came down and the walls closed in. I blacked out briefly, a slash of darkness flitting across my eyes. I found myself on one knee, choking, struggling for air.

My God, I thought, I'm dead. This is what death feels like. If you can't breathe, you're dead.

My eyes focused and then lost the capacity for definition as I zigzagged in and out of awareness, trying to understand what had happened.

Alex was standing over me with the blood-smeared butcher knife . . . but that blood had nothing to do with me . . . the faces peering down were a blur . . . I could feel rather than see everyone staring at me . . . what if that knife, dripping with someone's blood, was going to be used on me? . . . no, that was impossible . . . fear nevertheless spread through me . . . then the fear magically transformed itself into courage . . . I made it out the door and started down the stairs . . . my right leg felt numb . . . unzipping my jacket, I saw blood oozing over the loops of my belt . . . I pulled my shirt out of my pants . . . blood gushing from my insides . . . I could also feel warm blood running down my leg . . .

Now I realized for the first time that it was my blood, that I had been stabbed, that the somebody who was being shot at was me.

Screaming, two prostitutes named Marsha and Alice came to my aid. Marsha had once attended my father's Sunday School. "Let's get you to a hospital," she said. I leaned on them as we made it to the last step and then to the car.

I was losing strength fast. The sensations pouring through me weren't similar to nodding out gradually on drugs, but like dying quickly, as if someone was about to pull a thick, black curtain over me—and that would be the end.

Strangely, I hadn't yet felt any pain. Again I sunk into a state of semiawareness and semidelirium.

The chicks were trying to get me inside the car . . . here s

Alex only a few steps away from me . . . one hand in his jacket pocket . . . hand snapped out and holding a black revolver . . . "Ruud, I'm going to finish you right now" . . . beautiful, I thought, looking straight into the gun barrel . . . "pull the trigger. I have nothing to live for anyway" . . . there he was dead center in the barrel, real as sin, handsome, sleek, and sly with a sneer on his face . . . flames in the barrel of the gun, yellow, red, and blue . . . standing at the door of a super-enormous open furnace . . . my old idol, the Devil . . . someday perhaps I'd find out why Alex didn't shoot me and why he was in the car now beside me, the chicks sobbing in the back seat . . . Alex was clearing a path through the hospital's emergency room, into a bed . . . straps tying me down . . . everybody gone but Alex . . . "Hey, man, give me a tab" . . . Alex putting some water in a paper cup from the sink . . . holding my head while I dropped the speed . . . "Hey, man, we're still going on that caper. Just have to get sewed up a little and I'll be okay. Then we'll hit the creamery. Ten grand, maybe fifteen." . . . "Sure, kid, sure" . . . Still can't believe Alex cut me. He's my best friend . . .

The delirium gave way to excruciating pain. I saw a bottle of blood above my head. There were tubes in me. I was getting a transfusion. That was probably the reason I hadn't felt any pain. Too much narcotics in my bloodstream. But with the transfusion, every nerve in my body felt raw. I screamed and cursed God, cursed the doctors and nurses as the torrent of torture immersed me. I bit my tongue and could feel blood running from my mouth.

My mind swept back to Reverend Kennedy and his prophecy outside Dad's church—*If you don't get right with God now, you're going to wish you had. If you don't get right, something dreadful is going to happen to you in the next few days.* And then a band of angels began singing . . .

> Let the water and the blood,
> From Thy wounded side which
> flowed . . .

92

The anesthetic wore off while I was on the operating table. I came to and saw clamps on my stomach, a bright light burning above me, people around me in surgical gowns.

And there was Dad and Dave—both weeping. I had never seen my brother cry before.

"Pastor Ruud, I don't think your son's going to make it," a voice said. "The puncture is in the right abdomen, a double laceration of the colon, severe bleeding from the iliac vein. We're doing all we can."

"Brian! Brian!" Dad's face was urgent. "Ask God to help you! Ask God to forgive you! Tell Him you're sorry!"

"Lord, forgive me, oh please, forgive me. God, save my life for Dad's sake."

Then a rubber mask was fitted over my face, and a thick, black curtain fell, shrouding me in darkness.

8

"One Path Leads to Paradise, but a Thousand to Hell"

> *And why beholdest thou the mote that is in thy brother's eye, but considerest not the beam that is in thine own eye?*
>
> MATTHEW 7:3

> *The Pharisees said unto his disciples, Why eateth your Master with publicans and sinners? But when Jesus heard that, he said unto them, They that be whole need not a physician, but they that are sick.*
>
> MATTHEW 9:11–12

The darkness didn't turn to light again for three days. I awoke feeling more physically and mentally wasted than ever before, at the nadir of my life.

Emotion drumfired through me—fear, hatred, self-pity, guilt, every emotion but love. I vaguely remembered my deathbed plea to God, but He hadn't forgiven me. Else why would I feel so much pain, why this further taste of hell? Satan was still with me, my silent nurse.

My body felt like the scorched and seared target of a flame-thrower. Everything ached and burned, my head, jaws, cheeks, neck, shoulders, legs, even my teeth. Most of all my abdomen ached, my right side an exploding grenade. I was akin to a wounded pig in a slaughterhouse waiting for the last merciful blow that would send me into oblivion. Swathed in bandages, tube-fed, bedpan-ridden, I could barely move or talk.

My first visitors were Mom and Faithe. "This is my son," I heard Mom declare to heaven. "The doctor says he may die, but I won't let him die. Dear God, don't let him die."

Then I lapsed into unconsciousness.

When I came to, amazed that I was alive, my doctor was in the room. Introducing himself, he looked vastly more cheerful than I felt. Dr. Robert W. Cram had used his surgical skill to save my life. In the process, he had put his career in jeopardy.

Without braggadocio, he explained that there hadn't been time to wait for my father's arrival at the hospital to sign the written form giving him permission to perform an emergency operation on a minor. I had been minutes away from dying, so he proceeded with the surgery. No power on earth, he said, could have kept my father from barging into the operating room, though it was against all the hospital's rules.

"If I had died, I guess you'd be finished."

Dr. Cram shrugged, not pretending he was a hero. I liked him, he was a cool dude with glinting eyes and a handsome, relaxed face.

"You suffered a very deep wound," he said, "five and a half inches, from your stomach almost to your backbone. I'm afraid you'll carry a scar the rest of your life."

My doctor had saved a life, I thought, not worth saving. Had the prayers of Mom and Dad also helped?

"How long before I can leave?"

"Six weeks—minimum, if there's no infection."

But intestinal infection did set in, and he had to operate again.

After that, slowly, I began to show signs of improvement. During my convalescence, I became something of a hospital curiosity, a horrible example. "This is what a real doper looks like," I overheard a nurse say. Strange faces would peer into my room and shake their heads sadly.

When Dad and Reverend Kennedy came for a visit, I was happy to see them. The young preacher was smart and sensitive enough not to remind me of his fulfilled prophecy. Nothing had to be said aloud. His all-too-accurate forecast of my fate was in the back of both our minds.

"You must renounce sin forever," Dad implored me. "You must change your life, live for God. The Lord spared you for this one last chance."

As he dried his moist eyes, he added, "There's a policeman guarding your room. An anonymous tip was phoned into the station. The police know what happened, and now they think Alex Cordova may make another attempt on your life."

I remembered Alex giving me the speed before I blacked out. I still didn't really understand why he had stabbed me or why he hadn't killed me when he had the chance, why he had followed his mayhem with a complete about-face toward mercy. He had, after all, driven me to the hospital. Now he wanted to kill me again? The reasoning and behavior of a doper, myself included, was always predictably unpredictable.

"I want you to swear out a complaint against this monstrous Alex Cordova," Dad said. "Until you do, the police can't arrest him."

I knew the fix I'd be in if I signed. If Alex didn't get me, one of his dudes would. But Dad was right—he was a monster. I had done none of the things that Alex and the others had accused me of doing. Who but a monster would cut his best friend, consign him to an agonizing hospital bed, to the brink of death? He hadn't even asked to hear my side of it, he stabbed me without allowing me a single word of explanation. He had acted as judge, jury, and executioner.

97

I nodded, Dad called the guard, and I put my signature on the complaint. The words *Assault With Intent to Kill* leaped at me from the very formal, very official-looking document.

If convicted, Alex was facing a big fall. Maybe ten years in the pen. And when I testified against him, it was certain he would be convicted.

"Now, Brian," Dad said, "will you pray with us?"

"Yes."

Dad and Reverend Kennedy bowed their heads and sought my rescue and rejuvenation from God. When their prayer was completed, I said, meaning it, "Amen."

I was genuinely determined to change, to live right. I began my new life the day I left the hospital by throwing away my cigarettes. I was never going to touch dope again. For me now, crime was only a word in the dictionary and for all I cared, Little Chicago might as well be Outer Mongolia. I was finished with that scene.

Mom and Faithe were nursing me back to health. But five days after leaving the hospital I had another setback. My entire system became blocked, making it impossible to emit wastes. My stomach suddenly swelled like a balloon. I never dreamed that my taut, skeletal frame could take that much swelling without bursting. I was rushed back to the hospital for a third operation, which was successful. Soon my body was functioning normally and in a week I was allowed to go home.

Razor-thin, little more than a human bone pile, I couldn't sit down for more than five minutes without the uneasy sensation that my ribs were about to puncture my skin. I scarcely ate, unable to digest meat or potatoes, only small quantities of fruit, juices, and soup.

For two weeks I stayed clean of drugs, smoking, and drinking. I didn't even take an aspirin or a cup of coffee because of the caffeine, an alkaloid stimulant which was a mild but habit-forming drug. I stubbornly refused to get hooked on anything again.

The life of abstinence and discipline, I found, was not without its rewards. I was hardly an avid Christian, but then the flames of my rebellion and multifarious sins had been damped.

I allowed myself to look to the future optimistically, contemplating how I could continue growing in the Lord and how I wanted to spend the rest of my life. I considered returning to school so that I could acquire a skill I could sell to an employer.

On a dark, rainy Saturday afternoon, I was alone in the house—Dave and Faithe were with their friends and my folks had gone to the bedside of a sick parishioner to pray with him. I was dozing on the couch, something inane growling low from the TV set, when I was roused by the spanking of a car horn against my eardrums. Through the front-room curtains, I saw Alex and the other four from the stabbing fracas. There was no point in running. I was almost relieved to see them. I had expected this visit and was glad that the strain of the confrontation would soon be over. I had no plans as to how I would contend with Alex's predictable anger. Maybe God would consider me worthwhile enough by now to see me through this crisis.

Not wanting them to shove their way in and bust up my folks' place, I pulled on a sweatshirt and went outside.

Alex exuded a cordial lethality as he bluntly came to the point. "You got a bad deal, Brian, but you should know better than to squeal to the cops like some frightened, runny-nosed kid. I'm out on heavy bail. I don't have to tell you I can't allow you to testify against me." Smiling, he added, "Why don't we go for a ride and talk things over?"

Alex waved his head toward the car and his dudes pushed me into the back seat. Now I knew how David must have felt going up against Goliath, except I didn't even have a sling and a stone to defend myself.

Alex was Sphinx-quiet as the car proceeded beyond the city limits.

One dude said, "We're taking you on a far-out trip, man."

The brazenness of their rolling up to my house, abducting me in daylight, proved they were desperate, proved they meant business.

I was frightened, but I couldn't keep from wondering how long it would take before my body was found in the ditch that ran alongside the tomb-quiet country road where the car now ground to a halt. Alex's silence was more ominous than threats, silence that said my death was a foregone conclusion, the only detail left was the act of murder itself.

One of the dudes went to the trunk and snapped it open. My God, I thought wildly, they've even brought shovels and they're going to bury me right here in unholy ground. My body would never be found. Down the years my folks would have the additional burden of guessing what had become of me, why I'd disappeared at a moment when my full resurrection seemed so promising. All their lives, they would never give up hope . . . I knew they would keep an eye cocked on the front door waiting for me to walk in, fan through the daily mail for a word from me that I was alive and well. Theirs would be a long, unbearable punishment, but there was nothing I could do to prevent it.

Not shovels, but a case of booze emerged from the trunk. A couple of bottles were opened.

There was a quick, radical change in mood and atmosphere, grimness transposed to laughter. As I sagged helplessly and forlornly against the car, Alex offered me a drink.

"No," I said, "why not get it over with?"

"Get what over with?" Alex grinned. "Hey, you didn't think we were going to kill you? You've seen too many gangster movies." Then his voice held for a pregnant beat. "We're not going to kill you—unless we have to."

"For what it's worth, I want you to know I never double-crossed you."

"I realize that, kid. That's why I wanted to talk to you sensibly. How about teaming up again? We had some great times together, you have to admit that."

It was going unpredictably better than I had dared to hope. Alex was offering me a reprieve.

"You look kind of rough," he said. "Why don't you drop this and put your feet on the ground?" In his left palm was a tab of speed.

My soul cried out *no*. My heart and reason and mind also

100

said *no*. But something familiar, cynical, and tired surfaced in me, a voice saying *yes*.

I took the tab, letting it float down my throat on a surfboard of bourbon.

It wasn't long before the six of us were freaked out, shouting our undying loyalty to each other . . . all for one and one for all . . . let bygones be bygones . . . pals forever.

I was on the roller coaster again, hooked again—worse than before.

But at least the speed and the booze conked out the shrapnel of pain in my abdomen.

And I was alive. Or was I?

9

The Last Caper

*Ye shall not steal, neither deal
falsely, neither lie one to another.*

LEVITICUS 19:11

The Cordova-Ruud axis was reconstituted. Our gang,
which turned out to be an extremely loose confederation, went
on a four-month rampage, into everything in Saskatoon that
might bleed a dishonest dollar.

We seldom capered as a group. Everyone was more or less
doing his own thing. But we always rendezvoused at Alex's pad
(where I was living again) to divide the loot and party.

I became a hustler with two chicks working for me. Alex and
I rented a vacant joint on the West Side and set up our own
bootlegging operation complete with back-room gambling, most
of which was crooked. We hired two grifters to run the games,
experts in the use of weighted dice and marked cards. We also
went back to pushing stiffs (stealing and forging checks and
paying chicks to go to the bank to cash them for us). For kicks
we'd randomly thumb through the phone book and call a num-

103

ber. If there wasn't any answer, we'd head out to the address and scoop the house. Alex and I had become a pair of maniacs, game for anything, and we both were constantly turned on with any type of pill that happened to be handy.

Alex came back to the pad one evening boiling with rage. Flagged down for speeding, he'd lost his temper and hit the bull. He'd spent two hours in the bucket until his attorney could arrange bail. He was charged with assault and obstructing a peace officer.

Several months after Alex's scrape with the bull, the day was at hand for my appearance in court to testify against him. Since my reprieve from being murdered on that country road, we hadn't discussed the stabbing.

But now Alex warned me. "Be sure you don't foul up. Be very, very careful what you say."

Despite our closeness, Alex was taking no chances. For added intimidation and emphasis every dude and chick who'd been present when I was stabbed was at the door of the courtroom. No less than five of Alex's buddies told me that I'd be killed if Alex was convicted. They followed me into the courtroom and sat watching and waiting. Also watching and waiting was Dad, whom I hadn't seen or called since my last disappearance from home.

As I was summoned to the witness stand, I knew it was useless to tell the truth, even if I suffered a last-minute pang of conscience and wanted to blurt out what had actually occurred. My testimony would find no corroboration from anyone who had been there that night. Alex had more than a dozen of his acolytes ready to swear I was a liar. Whoever had phoned the anonymous tip to the bulls and told them of the stabbing wouldn't dare appear publicly.

I swept my eyes over the courtroom, aware that God and the Devil were both watching me—Dad, alert and anxious, Alex, hawk-eyed and glowering.

My exchange with the prosecutor was over in less than five minutes.

"Mr. Ruud, please tell the court how you were stabbed."

"It happened at a party. I'm sure it was an accident."

"Did Alex Cordova stab you?"

"I can't truthfully say he did."

"We have your signature on a complaint in which you state that the defendant was the person who knifed you."

"I signed that in the hospital while I was very weak. I was unable to think clearly. I was so sick I nearly died. I was pressured into signing."

"Did Mr. Cordova stab you or did he not?"

"When I was in the hospital, I honestly believed he had. But now that I've had all these months to think it over, I can truthfully and honestly say that I couldn't swear that Alex Cordova was the one who stabbed me."

Before throwing the case out, the judge threatened to charge me with perjury. But I knew he couldn't make it stick.

"Brian," Dad said after the adjournment, "I am at a loss for words. You are hopeless. A common, cheap liar and thief. For more than five years you've constantly been in serious trouble. What you just did in that witness box is an abomination in the sight of God. You've caused us nothing but heartache, shame, and disgrace. People won't come to my church because of you. Do me one favor. I want you to leave Saskatoon. I'll pay your plane fare to any city you want, but you've got to get out of our lives."

Dad's invitation to split town shook me up a little, but I said nothing, moving past him to the entrance of the courtroom where Alex was waiting to congratulate me for playing it smart.

Our partnership resumed, but it was short-lived. About a month later, Alex was sentenced to a solid year at Prince Albert on the assault and obstructing a peace officer beef. The law had finally collared him.

That really shook me up.

Whatever cohesion had existed in my life was gone. With Alex in prison, our bootlegging and gambling operation ended because I couldn't finance it alone. I also quit hustling, never having much taste for that type of action. I had no choice now but to caper alone—and I was looking for a big score.

I considered reviving the creamery heist. But that was a two-man job, and I doubted that I could crack both those safes alone.

While I had been in the hospital, I'd noticed that the pharmacy did a land-office business. In that establishment there would be the two commodities I wanted most—cash and drugs.

The night of the job I stole a Volkswagen—this time I wasn't going to be caught through the identification of my car. I wheeled the bug to a quiet street a block from the pharmacy and parked, leaving the ignition on for a fast take-off if that became necessary. I hurried on foot toward the hit, toward what would prove my last caper, toward that which would also put me in a Prince Albert cell and lead to my being caged in the Hole.

The pharmacy was on the ground floor. I had timed my arrival perfectly. The watchman went by—and I knew he wouldn't return for twenty-eight minutes.

In my belt under my jacket were the tools I'd need. I used a glass cutter to remove the safety glass quietly and efficiently. I'd guessed right—no burglar alarm. The screen was much more difficult to remove. I'd stupidly forgotten my wire cutters. I pried the screen loose with a crowbar but I had to bend, tug, and pull, finally removing most of it except for several jagged edges. As I slipped in, my hair caught on the edges of the screen. For a moment, I couldn't move. I jerked my head severely, untangling and freeing myself, but leaving a few strands of my hair imbedded in the screen. I thought of taking my lighter and burning the hair away—it could be a formidable clue if I became a suspect—but the flame might attract attention. Better to do it later.

Yawning before me was a cornucopia—drugs of every kind, including morphine, Demerol, and three cases of Desbutals—stashed on shelves, in cabinets, and in boxes.

I emptied six boxes of tissue paper and piled the stuff into them. There was still some room, so I looked for more booty. I shone my flashlight on one shelf holding a raft of pill bottles. The labels read: "Dispensing without prescription prohibited by Federal Law." I didn't recognize the name of the pills, but assumed they must be especially valuable. I scooped almost the entire shelf.

I busted open the cash register on the counter. There wasn't anything in it. Why lock it if it's empty? Then I slipped the lock on a cabinet, which contained several bottles of medicinal brandy. I drank what amounted to several shots.

I looked around for more valuables, spotting two white smocks on a coat rack. One of them yielded two twenty-dollar bills. Just then I heard a noise, a jangling of keys coming close.

I held my breath and the noise passed.

I slithered out through the window, went to the Volkswagen and backed it up to the pharmacy window. Noting the time, I figured I had about seven minutes before the watchman returned.

I managed to get all six boxes into the car. Altogether I estimated my haul would be worth thousands of dollars on the street. I drove to a big garage on a vacant lot rented by a friend of mine. I undid the padlock, wheeled inside, and climbing a ladder to the attic, I carried the boxes up one by one.

I dumped my burglar's tools and physician's gloves into a six-foot pit of grease and returned to the car. A large number of pills had spilled from their bottles and were scattered on the floor of the back seat. I looked for some sort of container in which to place the pills. Finding nothing, I remembered an old camper behind the garage that I had used several times to hide out from the bulls, to crash when coming down off drugs. I took my pillow case and dumped the stray pills and bottles into it, also hauling it to the attic and placing it among the rafters with the other stash.

Then I drove the car back to the spot from which I'd stolen it. Next I went to a pay phone and called for a taxi and had the cabbie drop me off at my car.

I moved on to the legger's, where a booze party was in full swing. There'd been another crackdown on narcotics, and the streets were bare.

"Hey, Ruud, got any stuff?" The request was from a pusher I knew, a fat dude with a pencil mustache. "I'll pay double the usual price."

"No, man," I said, "I'm dry." I didn't want to reveal my haul for a while because once the pharmacy job was discovered, the heat would be heavy. If word got back to the bulls that I had a big supply, they would come looking for me. I'd be a natural suspect.

But the two tabs I'd dropped on the drive down to the legger's were making me somewhat reckless. I called out to the dopers, "Downers! Uppers! Free! Come and get 'em!" I threw dozens of the capered pills that I'd stuffed into my pockets into the air. The heads scrambled after them like kids going for jellybeans. I laughed myself silly.

The party lasted two days and nights, and then finally I got tired of supplying the pills free. The pusher's offer of twice the normal price was looking better and better. "If you've got what you say you've got," he said when I discussed it with him again, "I can give you up to three thousand dollars." I knew the stuff would bring more, much more, if I took the trouble to push it myself. But I could always make another hit, and I'd hold back enough for my own use for at least six months and have the money as well. I accepted the deal.

I went back to the garage. Being super-careful, I hired a cab, stopping two blocks away. Though I was sure no one had followed me from the pharmacy to my hiding place, I scrutinized the area carefully on foot. There wasn't a soul in sight.

I went inside the garage and chained the door. With my flashlight, I headed up the ladder to the attic. Another few moments and I'd be on my way to the waiting pusher.

But after climbing five rungs, I could make no further progress up the ladder. There was an invisible barrier barring my way! An unseen presence on the ladder was holding me back. Invisible, unseen—yet real.

I climbed down, waved the flashlight around the garage and along the ladder. Nothing. It was spooky. Maybe I was freaking out. I had as little faith in ghosts as I did in God. This was ridiculous, I thought, as I started up the ladder again. But again it happened. The unseen presence wouldn't let me climb more than a few rungs. The attic now was a country mile away, impossible to reach.

Furious and confused, I dropped to the floor, thinking if I got a breath of fresh air maybe my head would clear and I could recover my stash. Then I heard the door being kicked and pounded.

"Open up," a voice commanded, "this is the police."

10

Still a Stranger to Myself

*And the Lord God said unto
the serpent, Because thou hast
done this, thou art cursed.*

GENESIS 3:14

*My transgression is sealed up
in a bag, and thou sewest up
mine iniquity.*

JOB 14:17

"Ruud, we should have guessed it was you. We've got
you now," a sergeant said, while another frisked me. "You're going
to be off the street for a long while. You'll be seeing your buddy
Cordova again shortly."

They didn't find any drugs on me, but the man who owned the
garage went looking for car parts in the attic and found the dope.
He immediately phoned the police about it. A dozen bulls sweep-
ing through the garage quickly located all my stash. *They* had no
trouble climbing the ladder.

I denied everything, trying to lie and con my way out of it. But the bulls would have none of it. They snapped handcuffs on me, and with a bull on each side, I was driven to the bucket.

The caper had proved a disaster.

I'd made more mistakes than a blind painter, pushed by an amalgam of speed, avarice, and anxiousness to score big without adequate planning. Forgetting my wire cutters was one incriminating error. My fingerprints were all over the scooped bottles, and strands of my hair still entangled in the screen. I'd forgotten to remove them, and the strands would certainly be found and used as evidence against me.

When we reached the jail, my pockets were emptied of all possessions—lighter, cigarettes, money, and wallet. Then another search for weapons and drugs, uncommonly thorough. Two bulls looked everywhere, in my shoes, the heels of my shoes, between my toes, in my teeth and ears as well as the less mentionable parts of my anatomy. But unless they decided to plant something on me, I was clean.

I was dumped into a cell, still drifting out on speed, a prelude to a fresh nightmare. In a few hours I was crashing down from my trip—and my body craved another tab, which was unobtainable. I was going cold turkey in the crowbar hotel.

The stab wound in my gut still tore at me. The floor tipped and swayed, my head swimming. It seemed as though I could pull my fingers from my hands, peel each off, drop them, and then watch them lie on the floor.

Free of an artificial high, forced to think, I felt, as I had most of my life, a stranger to myself.

I didn't know who or what I actually was, where I was going, what was going to happen next. Resentment, rage, and fear overtook me once more, swallowing me. I felt like Jonah going into the whale's belly. My movements were kinetic jerks, and I paced for what must have been hours, until a detective entered my cell. In a momentous formal monotone he read from a piece of paper. The three charges were heavy.

"Brian Douglas Ruud, nineteen years old, on this day you are

112

accused of possession of narcotics, a violation of Section three, Paragraph one of the Federal Narcotics Control Act.

"You are further accused of possession of stolen property over and above the sum of fifty dollars, a violation of Section two-ninety-six, Subsection A, of the Criminal Code.

"And you are also accused with breaking and entering with intent, a violation of Section two-ninety-two, Paragraph one, Subsection A, of the Criminal Code."

"What does it add up to?" I asked morosely.

"If you are convicted on all three counts and given the full penalty of the law"—he allowed himself a smile—"it adds up to thirty years in the penitentiary."

The shock of such a fate made me realize, for that moment at least, that the whole cheap, tawdry imitation of Capone had trailed off into a bummer. Big Al of Chicago had died at forty-eight, which was almost the exact age I'd be if I had to take the full rap, which I was sure I would.

My bail was set at five thousand dollars and I couldn't raise it. I used the one phone call I was allowed to call Dad. I wanted to plead with him to go my bail and give me one more chance to start anew. And that's when he disowned me—*I'm going to forget you were ever my son,* he said before breaking the connection.

I'd cried wolf once too often. If ever Dad meant business, he meant it this time. I couldn't blame him. I couldn't forgive him. Now I was alone and friendless, a freaked-out caricature of a human being.

I curled up in my cell, shivering, still undergoing the aftereffects of plummeting down from speed. My heart thumped so loudly I thought it was going to smash through my chest. Mercifully, I passed out.

The next day I was taken from the clammy cell. Guarded by a pair of bulls, we walked down the hallway, took the elevator upstairs and entered a small courtroom, where I was supposed to be officially charged.

I had seen a picture of the judge in the paper. Hard-featured

113

and forceful, he had a particularly rugged reputation for throwing the book at anyone involved in a drug offense.

"Step into the prisoner's box," the bailiff ordered.

I could support myself only by holding onto the rail. I thought I'd collapse at any moment. I knew I looked as wasted as I felt.

"This boy is apparently on drugs," the judge said. "He is not in fit condition. Return him to his cell for a week. Perhaps by then he'll be ready to make a civilized appearance before the court."

The next week was a cacophony of clanging cell doors, clanking keys, moaning prisoners, and delirium tremens yells all night long from the drunk tank.

A dude in the cell next to me asked me to help him commit suicide. He was in for armed robbery, and wanted my aid in stealing a razor blade so he could cut his wrists. I talked him out of it, but lying awake on my thin mattress that night I seriously considered suicide myself for the first time. I was sorry I'd changed his mind. He and I would both be better off dead.

At my next appearance before the judge I was charged on the three counts. In lieu of bail, I was remanded to Prince Albert to await trial.

The prison was like a family reunion. Dozens of dudes I knew were doing time there. I got a chance to talk to Alex for a moment in the mess hall. He looked good, had gained a lot of weight, but I could tell he was still on drugs. "Got any extra tabs?" I asked. "I'll see what I can do," Alex said.

I soon found a new enemy—boredom. A prisoner as well as nature abhors a vacuum. Except for a brief exercise period and work with the mess hall serving gang, there was little to do.

A con named Oz Everett approached me with a plea. Since I had access to the kitchen, he wanted me to help scoop a knife so he could shiv a guard who'd been hassling him. Oz was barely five feet three and was in for shotgunning his wife to death. He'd then turned the gun on himself. Instead of being killed, the blast shattered his right shoulder and arm. Where his arm should have been, there was only a stump.

The law inside the walls demands that you are either with or against fellow cons. I couldn't really refuse Oz, and I didn't want to. I was anxious to see what would happen. But if I was caught scooping the knife, it was another serious offense that could be added to the charges already against me.

I stole it anyway. Less than an hour later, it was reported missing, and the entire prison was searched. The guards never found it. The blade was passed in a chain from con to con and finally to Oz.

Unable to get to the guard he wanted to kill, Oz used the knife in a vain escape attempt. He caught another guard by surprise, put the knife to his throat, but was billied into unconsciousness by two bulls who came up from behind. He was due for a trial on this beef, but it didn't matter much to him since he was a lifer.

An investigation began as to how the knife was secreted from the kitchen. The chief guard told me that I was under suspicion and that I'd best be careful. I ignored the warning.

By now I'd learned that drugs could be obtained through someone from the outside boosting the stuff in. A delivery was made to one con from the other side of the walls in a tube of toothpaste. I was asked to hide the stuff for several hours. I helped myself to two dexies before returning it.

The new trip helped relieve the monotony. But when I came down this time, I was desperate for more drugs, and the only way to get them on an assured basis was to get out of prison. I planned a kite over the walls—a letter that could be smuggled out.

I wrote a doper dude who owed me a favor. In my kite, I asked him to sell a number of my possessions which would almost meet the price of my bail. If he'd loan me the rest, I'd repay him double. Since prisoner mail was censored by the guards, I took the precaution—in case my letter was discovered—of omitting the fact that what I was asking him to peddle consisted of loot (portable TV's, tires, a small armory of handguns, and a stash of drugs I'd buried behind the bootleggers') that I'd stolen, but forgotten to fence.

Finished, I folded the kite carefully, put it in the bottom of my tobacco pouch, and gave it to the tier clean-up man who passed it to another con due for a visit from his wife. She'd mail it on the outside. But on his way to see his wife, he dropped the pouch, and the letter was found by a guard. I'd written a kite that never flew.

The incident was reported to the warden. That and my suspected complicity in stealing the knife led to his ordering me to solitary.

Then came the frightening walk past Death Row and the cage that was the Hole.

Then came my decision that I could only escape the mountainous, insoluble problems bedeviling me by taking my own life.

11

... A Wretch Like Me

With God all things are possible.

MARK 10:27

*For unto you is born this day
... a Saviour.*

LUKE 2:11

The spoon handle was now a knife, honed stiletto-
sharp during my reverie.

Legs crossed under the trunk of my body, I was sitting on the
frigid floor. But in moments I'd be in the place of everlasting heat.

Using my final ounces of energy, I raised the knife in my right
hand as high as I could to get as much downward thrust as possible when it tore into my left wrist. No point in looking for a
vein—your veins don't stick out when you're doing dope as
heavily as I was.

With so cool and lethal a shiv, one thrust should do it, one
thrust should spill a river of blood from my quaking skin.

The blade began its errand of mercy and peace. . .

Then, unexpectedly, I looked up and four guards rushed in. Instantly, one of them placed a perfect kick, sending the knife flying from my hand. It clattered to a halt at the opposite corner of the cell, out of reach.

The burly, unfriendly guard who'd been one of my escorts to the Hole said in a burly, unfriendly voice, "Ruud, I'd be delighted to make an exception in your case, but the Crown says it's part of our job to keep you alive."

"Why? Why couldn't you have waited one more lousy minute?"

"I almost wish we had," he added, walking over and retrieving the knife. "We suspected you'd try this. After working here a while, you can usually smell the cop-out cowards who want to do themselves in. You had that smell all over you. That's why we came by to check."

After combing my cage for other weapons of self-destruction, the guards left.

My suicide attempt, as everything else in my life, had been bungled. It was said among the cons in Prince Albert that after doing time in the Hole, no inmate was ever the same. Something happened to his mental processes; he was forever wounded, his emotions irrevocably scarred. A breathing man was never made to languish in a living tomb. Now I could understand what the cons meant. Whatever happened to me in the future, I too would never be the same. The Hole would forever be part of my nightmares and chill my waking hours.

Alone again and desolate, I still wanted to die. I thought of death now as going home, maybe not to the Devil, but to inch-thick steaks . . . strawberry pie and vanilla ice cream, homemade bread, hockey games. Since there was no rest in this world, there must be a place somewhere that was all-cool, all-beautiful, a trip beyond that was hassle-free, without pressure. A place where there were always good things to eat and enjoyable things to do sans drugs and cigarettes and booze and crime. A place where people were friendly and loved one another.

I longed for such a place, realizing as I fell asleep that if there were such a utopia, whoever stood at the entrance would slam the gate in my face.

I awoke to a rustling sound—the guard was sliding my next meal into my cell. This time there was no spoon with my bowl of soup.

A century of boredom stretched before me. One con, I remembered, had told me he'd read the Bible cover to cover during his stay in the Hole. It wasn't much of a book, he'd said, but it passed the hours.

"Hey, man," I asked the guard, "can I have a Bible?"

He looked at me with undisguised shock. "You're not going to turn religious, are you?"

"Shut up, man, I'd rather have a copy of *Playboy* and groove on the chicks. But a Bible's all I'm allowed—right?"

"Okay, but I'll be watching you," the guard replied. "We don't want a repeat performance—the last guy in here who asked for a Bible stuffed the pages down his throat."

He returned in a few moments, tossing the Book through the bars. Feeding time at the zoo, I thought.

Though I was the son of a preacher and the Bible was read and quoted constantly in my home, I'd never so much as opened the Book. My only knowledge of Scripture was from my oral Sunday School lessons and sermons I'd heard in church. I thought I might as well read it from start to finish, curious in a way to find out what my old man and all the world's religious nuts found so engrossing about the Bible. Besides, there wasn't anything else to do.

I opened the dog-eared Gideon to Genesis 1:1. "In the beginning God created the heaven and the earth." It went on through all the stories I'd heard in Sunday School, which hadn't impressed me then and weren't impressing me now.

By Chapter 10 Moses was into the generations of the sons of Noah, Shem, Ham, and Japheth . . . and then this dude began begetting that dude, on and on, through a lot of unpronounceable names.

119

It was a drag, a dork of a book. I couldn't make sense of any of it. So much for the Old Testament. I turned to the New Testament, knowing it wouldn't be exciting, but maybe a little more interesting.

"The Gospel According to Saint Matthew" was the heading in big black type on the first page. Who the heck was Matthew?

I started reading and I was introduced to this Jesus dude whose name was familiar to me only as a curse. It told, to my consternation, how He had a special birth—"Behold, a virgin shall be with child, and shall bring forth a son." That was too much. As I'd always suspected, the Bible only amounted to a collection of far-out fairytales. How could Mary conceive through something called the Holy Ghost, which I recalled Mom once telling me had filled her, but which I didn't understand. Then and there I would have thrown the Book aside if I'd had anything else to read.

Without an alternative and through sheer inertia, I kept going. Pretty soon, when Jesus was a young child, this fat cat, King Herod, didn't seem to be happy about His birth. He was so jealous that he wanted to kill Jesus. Though I'd almost murdered an infant when I was five years old, that was one escapade I'd later come to honestly regret. I hadn't known any better, of course, but a grown man putting out a contract on a helpless kid was real bad news. You dirty king, I thought.

Hey, I thought, what's happening?

Just like that I was rooting for this Jesus kid, and I was mad at Herod for trying to murder Him. I didn't know why or how—but I was on Jesus' side. I couldn't wait to find out how Jesus got out of it.

Then I read that an angel from God came to Joseph in a dream and warned him to split to Egypt with Jesus and Mary. When Herod found out, he blew his mind and ordered every child two years old and under in and around Bethlehem to be killed. Herod belonged on Death Row down the corridor from my cell. If I could be alone with him two minutes, I'd spit in his face and run a shiv through him. When Herod died, I wasn't sorry.

Next I went through the part about Jesus going from Galilee

120

to the Jordan River to be baptized by John the Baptist. Jesus had
to talk John the Baptist into it. Seemed like Jesus was too humble
a dude, and He had to come up a loser.

Next I came to a super-powerful passage, and I could see it like
it was happening before my eyes, like someone had put a huge
Technicolor screen into my cell.

> And Jesus, when he was baptized, went up straightway
> out of the water; and, lo, the heavens were opened
> unto him, and he saw the Spirit of God descending like
> a dove, and lighting upon him:
> And lo a voice from heaven, saying, This is my
> beloved Son, in whom I am well pleased.

It had been a long, long time since my Dad could say he was
well pleased with his son.

I continued grooving on these two super-dudes—God and
Jesus—doing Their thing. They were on Their own tear, but
unlike Alex and me They weren't capering for selfish reasons.
They were interested in giving people something—but what?

Now Jesus had a meeting with the Devil. Man, I hoped that
Satan wouldn't be able to push Jesus around. The Devil offered
Jesus all the kingdoms of the world, a super-haul. "All these
things will I give thee," the Devil said, "if thou wilt fall down
and worship me."

Jesus was cool, answering: "Get thee hence, Satan: for it is
written, Thou shalt worship the Lord thy God, and him only
shalt thou serve." The Devil took off, knowing he couldn't ram-
rod Jesus or tempt Him as he had me.

Jesus next became a preacher like my Dad and he was saying
the exact words I'd heard Dad say a thousand times, "Repent ye:
for the kingdom of heaven is at hand."

I was tripping along with Jesus every step of the way, hungry
now to find out more about His scene.

I read the Sermon on the Mount and the Golden Rule and
began to turn off a little. A lot of that was for suckers. Jesus
wouldn't last fifteen minutes in Little Chicago preaching stuff

121

like, "Lay not up for yourselves treasures upon earth, where moth and rust doth corrupt, and where thieves break through and steal: But lay up for yourselves treasures in heaven, where neither moth nor rust doth corrupt, and where thieves do not break through and steal."

He was hard to figure, this Jesus. One minute I was with Him, the next He lost me. The Devil had given Him a shot at scooping the whole world for Himself, and He flat-out refused. That took a lot of guts, especially since Jesus didn't seem to have a pair of nickels to rub together. All He was interested in was His Father and heaven.

Didn't He ever take a minute to relax? No parties, no chicks, no speed in His life? He seemed to coast along on a natural high. I wondered what He did for kicks—and then I found out.

Jesus met a leper, who worshipped Him. "Lord, if thou wilt, thou canst make me clean."

And in a split second the leper was clean and healthy and altogether. I was a leper, too, an untouchable to my folks, hated, feared, mistrusted by everyone, facing thirty years of imprisonment, committed to a living death as that leper had been facing a living death.

But Jesus had the power to lay His hand on him and give him a whole new life because the leper said he believed in Him as Lord.

Was it that easy? Could I say, *Jesus, I believe in you,* and would He heal me as he had the leper? Would He say, *Brian, be thou clean.*

No chance. The healing of the leper had occurred two thousand years ago. And the age of miracles was past. I'd never seen a miracle, and never expected to. Not even Jesus could cleanse *me.*

Though He couldn't do a thing for me, I was grooving on Him anyway. Now I understood how He got His kicks, what His true scene was. He just went around helping people. He could have walked right by that leper and thought, "Old man, you're a festering, disintegrating, pus hole of a monster. Split. I've got more important capers on my mind."

But Jesus didn't do that. He dropped what He was doing and

122

took pity and showed mercy to that freak and made him whole again.

Jesus *was* Superman, a super-cool soul Man. He was the Son of God, busy worrying about sin throughout the entire world, shouldering massive burdens. Still He stopped and took the time to heal one scroungy, mangy, woebegone leper.

And there was nothing in it for Him . . . or was there? Maybe Jesus put that leper together for His own selfish reasons to prove to all the skeptical dudes in Israel that He was super-special, that He was the genuine product, the true Son of God. Sure, that was it. He pulled off one quick miracle for one insignificant wretch, but He would never bother doing it again, He would never trouble to heal and help little people without clout or money. I knew that sooner or later Jesus would sell out to the fat cats. Even the Son of God had to have an angle. Everybody did when it came down to the bottom line. Jesus wouldn't be an exception.

I picked up the Book again and discovered I was wrong about Him.

Soon after healing the leper He wheeled all over the place helping other hopeless people who couldn't do Him a bit of good. He healed the centurion's servant of palsy and cured Peter's mother-in-law of a fever.

Then he began healing people wholesale, restoring health to what must have been as many psyched-out weirdos as there are in the patient population at a funny farm in today's world, many doomed to spend the rest of their lives as neurotics and psychotics —branded as such by psychiatrists.

I learned Jesus was a super-headshrinker, too. Matthew 8:16 said: "They brought unto him many that were possessed with devils: and he cast out the spirits with his word, and healed all that were sick."

I was a pillhead, possessed by the Devil. If only I'd had lived in biblical times I would have been in that crowd and He would have cast out the demon spirits from my body. What I needed was a time machine, like one I'd seen in science-fiction movies, to take me back to that day when He healed the many.

123

Man, what a dude this Jesus was turning out to be. His next caper was even more tremendous. He and His disciples were on a ship. A tremendous storm arose, waves so high everybody was going to drown.

"And his disciples came to him, and awoke him, saying, Lord, save us: we perish."

Jesus rebuked the winds and the sea, and everything was triple-cool.

"The men marvelled, saying, What manner of man is this, that even the winds and the sea obey him!"

What an idiot I was, comparing Jesus to Superman. Superman was only a paper comic strip invention—he was nothing compared to Him. Here was a dude both human and godly, barreling around Israel performing wonders. Here was a dude who was flesh and blood. He had eyes and ears, a nose, legs, He got tired and slept. He had problems and worries even though he was the Son of God and had supernatural powers.

No one had ever explained Him to me that way, that he was *real*. No one had ever explained the *real Christ*. The Christ of miracles. The Jesus of love. The Jesus who wouldn't turn anyone away, who wanted to help everybody. The Jesus who wanted to be everybody's friend. The real, living, personal Christ who met brutality with patience and kindness, who asked nothing for Himself but kept giving, giving, then giving more. He was a dude who wasn't hung up on number one. I couldn't believe He was that pure and selfless.

Suddenly my cell wasn't cold anymore. Suddenly it was invaded by a presence spreading warmth. Jesus was becoming real to me, floating up from those pages of Matthew. I could see Him only in my mind's eye, yet it seemed I could almost hear Him breathing. He was encapsulated inside my brain, ten feet tall.

Jesus was moving in on me and He was moving on to his next caper. I couldn't wait to find out more about Him. I clutched that Gideon Bible, continuing my trip with Him. I'd rather drop more Matthew than speed now, even if I could get my hands on a ton of tabs.

He healed another basket case, also sick with the palsy. "Son," He said, "be of good cheer; thy sins be forgiven thee."

Right then I longed for Jesus to walk into my cage and say to me, too, "Son, be of good cheer; thy sins be forgiven thee."

But what would Jesus be doing messing around the Hole at Prince Albert? Why would He stop to rap with me? And even if He forgave all my sins—and that would be a big chunk of forgiveness—I'd end up double-crossing Him, go right back to my old ways if and when the highly unlikely miracle occurred that I would somehow be set free to hit the street again. I'd double-cross Him as I had Dad and Reverend Kennedy after they'd prayed for me in the hospital.

There was no point in lying to myself. Cool as He was, Jesus was a life raft, a parachute, indispensable when facing death, big trouble, or hopelessness. But once He put you together it was natural to forget about Him as I would forget Him if he unstrung me, having used Him as I had used everyone else—for my own selfish ends.

Then again, I thought, how could I explain the new warmth in my cell, the gentle heat spreading through my body and mind. How explain that I didn't want to trip out on speed? How explain that I had come even this far with Jesus when my entire life was in conflict with everything He represented?

The explanation was easy. The cons who said hole time never left you the same were right. I was going stir crazy, hallucinating, suffering a flashback induced by all the drugs I'd taken. I was trapped with Jesus and the Bible because there wasn't anything else to read.

And there it was on the page—confirmation that I was on another bummer: "Neither do men put new wine into old bottles: else the bottles break, and the wine runneth out, and the bottles perish," Jesus said.

That was me, an old bottle, a teen-age washout and has-been.

But He added: "They put new wine into new bottles, and both are preserved." New wine?

That puzzled me until I read the next lines where Jesus dealt

125

out more super-miracles, raising from the dead the daughter of Jairus, who also worshipped Him. Then a woman who was diseased with an issue of blood for twelve years touched the hem of His garment. "Daughter," Jesus said, "be of good comfort: thy faith hath made thee whole."

He could do all that, I marveled, if faith was pledged to Him. I struggled hard to understand the nature of faith. And understanding came to me as I sped my way through the stories of the two blind men and Peter.

"Thou son of David, have mercy on us," the blind men cried out to Jesus.

"Believe ye that I am able to do this?" Jesus asked.

"Yes, Lord," they answered.

He touched their eyes, saying, "According to your faith be it unto you." From that moment those dudes had twenty-twenty vision.

"According to your faith be it unto you." Was that the answer, the wonder of it all? Faith given in exchange for a miracle? Was that what the Jesus trip was all about?

It seemed too easy, too pat. I still wasn't convinced as I put myself in the place of Peter, who was having as rough a time of it as I'd had when I was stabbed.

Peter and the other disciples were caught aboard a ship in a storm, and they were scared to death. "Jesus went unto them, walking on the sea, Be of good cheer; it is I; be not afraid."

But Peter and I were having the same doubts.

"Lord," Peter said, "if it be thou, bid me come unto thee on the water."

I put the Book down and tried to guess Jesus' next move. Peter was up against it. It was one thing for Jesus to walk on water, but Peter didn't have a chance of pulling it off. He'd need a rowboat or a frogman's suit to make it. If Peter was smart, he'd cool it and wait until Jesus came to him. Peter was only an ordinary dude, like me. He didn't have any supernatural power. Scratch one disciple. Not even Jesus could win them all.

"Come," Jesus said to Peter.

And that dummy Peter stepped into the water. He couldn't

even swim. The wind was boisterous as a Saskatoon winter and Peter began to sink.

Man, I thought, you've had it—you're finished.

"Lord, save me," Peter said fearfully.

"And immediately Jesus stretched forth his hand, and caught him, and said unto him, O thou of little faith, wherefore didst thou doubt?"

I was so excited now I tore through the rest of the Book at a breakneck pace, grooving on every episode. Man, I was turning into a Bible freak.

What a soul Man He was, healing the lame, blind, dumb, maimed. I was standing at His side as He fed five thousand from seven loaves of bread and two little fishes.

Now He was explaining the power of faith. "Verily I say unto you, If ye have faith, and doubt not . . . ye shall say unto this mountain, Be thou removed and be thou cast into the sea; it shall be done. And all things, whatsoever ye shall ask in prayer, believing, ye shall receive."

When I watched this innocent Jesus taken out in front of the mob, when a crown of thorns was placed on his brow, when they spat at him and mocked him, I wanted to kill every one of them. How could they do this to an innocent man, a man who had done nothing but good, a man who was now my friend? Didn't they see that he loved them and only wanted to give them a good life? But all of a sudden, chills ran up and down my spine. It was like Jesus spoke to me and said, "Brian, every time you light up a joint and go on a caper, every time you curse my name, you are standing with the mob, slapping me in the face and spitting at me along with the crowd."

Finally, I read, wide-eyed—and this was far and away the best part of the Jesus story—that He was sealed in a tomb, but three days later He split. An angel of the Lord rolled back the stone from the door of his tomb and said: "He is not here; for he is risen."

That meant Jesus was alive and well and altogether.

After his death and resurrection, Jesus met with his disciples and gave them The Great Commission:

All power is given unto me in heaven and in earth.
Go ye therefore, and teach all nations, baptizing them
in the name of the Father, and of the Son, and of
the Holy Ghost. Teaching them to observe all things
whatsoever I have commanded you: and, lo, I am
with you alway, even unto the end of the world. Amen.

I closed the Bible, and it fell from my hands to the floor of the
cell. I was so spaced out on Jesus I could barely contain my joy.
Speed had never given me a trip remotely approaching the high I
was now enjoying.

There was a waterfall of things to think about. It wasn't only
the words of Matthew, the stark, precise double columns of type
in the Bible that had reached and touched me. There was more,
much more. A *feeling* swept from those pages, a feeling that I
wasn't alone. A feeling that said for the first time in my life I
wasn't alone . . . that I had a new friend. It was strange and
wonderful. Maybe . . . just maybe Christ would take a little
of his time to heal me as He had the leper and all the others.

A voice ripped through me: "Don't get your hopes up," the
Devil said. "There's no way out for you. Christ escaped His tomb,
but you're not about to escape yours. You're going to stay buried
in the subterranean no-man's-land under Prince Albert."

"Okay, okay," I answered. "I know there's no way out, but I
still want to meet that super-cool soul Man. I've just walked the
shores of Galilee with Him and I think I have something to say
to Him, something He might like to hear."

Again it hit me that nobody had ever shown me this real, personal, vital Christ. I'd never heard anything like this in Sunday
School. Never read or heard Him preached as a ten-foot-tall
soul-saver. Never heard about Him being the living Christ, out
there commuting from heaven to earth, showering down His
blessings on the deserving . . . who for a pledge of faith would
scoop you away from the Devil.

I'd stumbled on a voyage of discovery, wondering as I held my
breath where the trip was going to take me now, if my trip was
going to spin into something of glory, something of splendor . . .
or flicker and die.

128

I knew I wasn't hallucinating, this wasn't a flashback. This was real. Already desire for everything except meeting Jesus was gone from me. I had no yearning for drugs or booze or chicks. I didn't want to caper.

That much was already new. It was too much to expect a total cleansing of my soul and spirit, of my mind and body.

All I wanted was a friend named Jesus who'd lived the greatest life ever, and *cared* as a friend should care. I was on my knees— praying honestly for the first time in my life, saying, as I closed my eyes:

"Hey, Jesus, it's Brian.

"If you're there, you know all about me, and I can't blame you if you're disgusted. But, Jesus, all I want from you is to be your friend. You're cool, super-neat, and maybe you and I could find a way to groove together. I'm not asking to get out of jail. I'm not asking to be acquitted. I deserve those thirty years they're going to give me. I'm not asking for anything, only your friendship.

"I've prayed before, but as a phony and a hypocrite. I turned my back on you every time. That was because I didn't understand you as I do now. But, hey, Man, let's be friends . . . that's all I'm asking.

"Jesus . . . I've . . . never . . . had . . . a . . . friend."

When I opened my eyes, there was silence in my cell. Then the strange feeling came over me again.

I couldn't see Him, but He was there anyway, walking down an endless tunnel from heaven. He stopped right above my cell.

Wait a minute, Jesus said in a voice that threaded gold to silver. *Listen. Somebody is calling me. Somebody needs me.* He was talking to one of his angels.

Now I heard the negative voice of the Devil again. *Jesus can't help you. It won't work. You'll fail again. You're a born loser. You won't stay clean of sin. You start messing with Jesus and your friends will laugh at you. You don't want to be a Jesus freak. Come on, Ruud, get tough. You're on your last legs, drowning like Peter. That's the only reason you prayed.*

"No . . . no . . . no!" I screamed. "I've listened to you before. I wanted to be a hood and look at me. One hundred and

129

eighteen pounds of concentrated misery. You've never been my friend. If you were a friend I wouldn't be wasting away in the Hole, wouldn't be almost dead. I wouldn't have disgraced and tortured my folks. I won't listen to you. You're nothing but a puddle of vomit."

Again the voice of gold threaded to silver: *There's that dope addict, thieving preacher's son. He's calling me.*

All at once I became the defendant in a court case. And the angel with Jesus was arguing against me.

He's a bad risk. He'll con and use you. He'll spit all over your Commandments like he's always done. Jesus, he isn't worth saving. Let's move on. Your schedule is too heavy to stay here another second.

Then—incredulously—Jesus said to the angel. *Silence.*

Here it comes, I thought—the verdict. The Judge of all Judges was going to pass sentence on me.

"Tell me, Jesus, tell me the verdict. Tell me I'm guilty and there's no hope."

Don't you see? Jesus said to the angel. *I love Brian, he needs me. I am going to give him eternal life.*

Then Jesus talked to me directly for the first time.

Brian, you are mine. I have chosen you. Today, right now, I am writing your name in The Book of Life which means that the verdict is life everlasting. You will never have to walk alone. I'll always be with you. I'll be your friend.

Tears gushed from my eyes and it was beautiful, almost unbearably beautiful. I was purified and healed and as I rose to my feet, I wasn't scared anymore. I felt showers of blessings, showers of joy, showers of love overwhelming me, super-heavy, super-neat, super-tremendous, and wonderful.

I wasn't a leper anymore . . . I'VE GOT IT! I'VE GOT JESUS! *Be thou clean* . . . I was shouting and singing . . . Grace, *Amazing grace! how sweet the sound* . . . Ecstasy . . . *Lo, I am with you alway, even unto the end of the world* . . . Somebody say amen for Brian Ruud . . . *That saved a wretch like me!* . . . Glory to Jesus, the real Christ . . . *I once was lost, but now am found* . . . I couldn't take anymore. How could anyone cry and whoop and shout and sing all at the same time? . . . *Was blind, but now I see* . . . Thank you, Jesus, thank you for the super-trip . . . Oh, Jesus, thankyouthankyou thankyou . . . *Whatsoever ye shall ask in prayer, believing, you shall receive* . . . I was dipping, hooting, whipsawing, diving, tripping, sliding around my cell . . . *When we've been there ten thousand years* . . . BORN AGAIN . . . SUPER-COOL SOUL MAN, thank you, Jesus, and praise your precious name . . . *Be of good cheer; it is I; be not afraid* . . . I couldn't come down.

> When we've been there ten thousand years,
> Bright shining as the sun,
> We've no less days to sing God's praise
> Than when we first begun.

Finally the euphoria ended and, exhausted, I sat down on the cement ledge.

Brian! Jesus said. He hadn't split, He was still with me. *I want you to preach in my name, preach my Word.*

"Dear Jesus, ask anything of me. But I can't preach. I'm nothing. I don't even have an education."

I don't care about your education.

"I'll fail."

If you do, it won't be the first time.

"Do you want me to spend the next thirty years preaching to a bunch of cons?"

They need me as much as you did, all of them.

"Yes, Jesus. All right. If that's what you want, I'll preach."

Then He was gone, replaced by the guard who I hadn't heard approaching my cell. There must have been a gleam and a luminescence about me, otherwise the guard would never have said, "Ruud, you look like you've seen an angel!"

"I don't care if you believe me or not. But you hit it right. I did see an angel . . . and Jesus just walked in."

The guard took off like a flash of lightning.

About ten minutes later he was back with five other guards— and the warden. Hallelujah! My first congregation.

131

12

"On Behalf of Her Majesty the Queen Against Brian Douglas Ruud"

Therefore if any man be in Christ, he is a new creature: old things are passed away; behold, all things are become new.

II CORINTHIANS 5:17

"I'm told you've seen Jesus," the Warden said, staring at me hard, carefully, with a mixture of suspicion and astonishment. "Your eyes are shining, they're glowing, you have an otherworldly appearance about you. In twenty years of running this institution, I've never encountered anything like this. Did you really see God?"

"I'm not sure. I think I saw Him as much as anyone has ever seen Him since His death and resurrection. It's difficult to describe what happened. But whether I saw him or not, I sure *felt* Him, no mistake about that."

Through the bars I offered the warden that life-changing Gideon Bible. This was as good a time as any to preach my first sermon and win my first convert.

"That super-soul Man who walked the shores of Galilee stepped right out of this Book and walked into my life. Warden, how would you like Him to step out of this Book, walk into your life, and turn you on, too?"

He and the guards backed away, still suspicious, still awestruck.

"Fine, Ruud, fine," the warden said as all of them split. "You just stay in there and keep praying."

Funny, I thought, where did he think I might go? I was still Hole bait, and had no idea when I'd get out. It didn't matter, though. I felt freer than any con in the joint, freer than anybody outside the walls.

November 25, 1965—the hallowed day on which I was saved and reborn. Good-bye Capone, hello Christ. Good-bye death, hello life. From a bum trip to the trip beyond.

"For God so loved the world, that he gave his only begotten Son, that whosoever believeth in him should not perish, but have everlasting life," I read, eagerly continuing my study of the Bible. "He that believeth in him *is not condemned*."

I learned that a lot of the heaviest dudes in the Bible had been busted. Not only Christ, but Peter and John. Paul was almost busted on one occasion in Jerusalem because his bold witnessing for the Lord aroused so much anger against him. He split and hid out in Tarsus for years. But that didn't break his spirit.

And the Hole wasn't going to break my spirit either. I didn't care if they never released me.

A new preacher had to practice, and he had to practice wherever he happened to be. I began composing sermons and committing as much Scripture as possible to memory. I preached and preached and preached—to the steel bars, to the walls, to Jesus. And I preached to the guard whenever he came around with my vitamins and soup, a few scant pieces of macaroni and noodles swimming in the watery slop. But I no longer considered it slop. In my new kingdom, every meal was a banquet.

Usually I ignored the food, trying, without success, to win the guard to Christ. Though he wouldn't give his heart to Jesus, I could tell from his attitude that his respect for me had grown. He was also somewhat frightened of me. I'd already learned that there was nothing more frightening to the unsaved than a zealous new child in Christ and that the challenge for the newborn would be to stay turned on for the rest of his life.

I came up with a mass escape plan—a jailbreak that would freak out the world. ENTIRE INMATE POPULATION OF PRINCE ALBERT PRISON ESCAPES, the headline would read. Man, what a blast.

The escape plan was to convert every con in the joint to Jesus. Then they could share with me the true understanding of freedom. They would escape drugs and booze, be free of the desire to commit the robberies and scams and murders that many were planning after they were paroled. I wanted to make every con a soldier of the cross instead of a soldier of crime.

The prison doctor came in, a stocky dude with a serious mien. "I understand you've had a . . . well . . . you've been seeing things."

"You might say that."

"Mr. Ruud, I'm aware that it's not impossible for even a prisoner in solitary confinement to obtain drugs. I promise no reprisals if you tell me the truth. What drugs have you been taking?"

"Matthew, Mark, Luke, and John, Acts and Revelation," I said, laughing.

"Considering the circumstances in which you find yourself, you seem abnormally happy."

"I am. I'm super-happy. Doc, do you know Jesus? Do you know the real Christ?"

"I'm not here to discuss religion."

"Well, you should be. That's the only thing 'wrong' with me."

"Mr. Ruud, to be perfectly blunt, there isn't a mental institution in Canada or the United States that doesn't have its resident Jesus and patients who claim direct communion with God."

"I can only speak for myself, and if you're saying I'm crazy, maybe I am. Crazy with love for the Lord."

135

"I'm sorry, but there's no medical explanation for your highly irregular and uncommon change in behavior. It isn't . . . uh . . . normal."

"Normal or not, I've never felt better."

When that dude left, I was sure he still thought I'd flipped out.

I knelt to pray a prayer to Jesus for being so cool, to thank Him for what I'd been given. In a moment, I could feel Him again, coming closer . . . closer . . . closer . . . like a great big star had slipped out of orbit and into my cell.

My body shook and tears ran down my face.

I was sure I was going to heaven, that Jesus had come to call me home. I praised Him . . . and praised Him. He came closer.

Then I became frightened. There was so much power in the cell that if one more teaspoon had been added that steel cage would have crumbled and buckled. I was lifted out in space, coasting on a new trip, floating, shouting endless hallelujahs and amens, praising Jesus.

And then I was speaking in tongues, worshipping Jesus in heavenly language exactly as the Bible related in Acts 2 & 4—

> And suddenly there came a sound from heaven as of a
> rushing mighty wind, and it filled all the house where
> they were sitting. And they were all filled with
> the Holy Ghost, and began to speak with other tongues,
> as the Spirit gave them utterance.

The words that fell from my mouth weren't in the unabridged *Webster's,* wonderful, dancing, leaping, precious, holy words. Jesus was closer to me this time than He had been when I was saved. Imbedded in the heavenly language was food from His supernatural force and I feasted with unquenchable hunger.

It lasted five or six minutes—until I heard the bars on my cell rattling and saw the guard standing outside, gaping. He thought I was crazy, too. But it didn't matter what anyone thought except Jesus.

I remembered Mom telling me how she and Dad had been filled. I had felt the same electricity. I had also been baptized with the Holy Ghost.

136

"All right, Ruud, we're sending you back to your regular cell," the guard said.

At first I didn't want to leave—in a sense I would be leaving Jesus. Then I realized that Jesus was everywhere and that I had a great deal of work to do for Him.

I didn't bother to ask how long I'd been in the Hole—a day, a week, a month. The amount of time spent there was of no consequence—what was important was that I'd found the Savior, my forever friend, in one of Prince Albert's steel and cement cages.

I had come in a would-be suicide, I was leaving with a guarantee of everlasting life. I had entered a prisoner of hell, and was emerging a captive of Christ. I had been tattered, tired, tapped out, but was departing transfigured. Those who said a con never left the Hole in the same shape in which he entered were right.

Then and now, I've never been anywhere as glorious as the Hole. A day never passes without my thinking of that underground chamber of horror that became a chamber of wonder. I often miss it and wonder if Christ is still there turning on others to the trip He gave me.

The door of the Hole swung open, and I walked out a free man, looking forward to spending the next three decades preaching in prison. That was going to be my ministry for Jesus.

The shower and clean clothes felt wonderful.

As I was escorted back to Block G, Cell 12, a lot of the cons ribbed me good-naturedly. The news of what had happened to me in the Hole had spread throughout the joint.

Dinner was another banquet—soup, bread, turnips, and hamburger. I read my Bible until lights out at 7:45 P.M. but sleep eluded me for hours as I struggled with a sudden, heavy craving for a cigarette.

I told myself that the Lord would understand that as a freshman Christian I couldn't be perfect right away. One cigarette won't do any harm. I flicked my lighter to a flame. As I did so, I heard a great choir of singing angels and once again the voice of Jesus.

Did I save you to violate the temple of your body?

Then I knew I didn't need cigarettes. I tossed them through the bars, never to smoke again after years of consuming two to three packs a day. Out through the bars also went my desire for drugs and crime and unholy sex. Sin became a stranger to me from that moment.

I put my head to the pillow and fell asleep at four A.M., waking at six, feeling completely refreshed.

"Lord, what do you want me to do today?" I said the moment I woke up.

The answer came as I was walking along the tier. I found myself coming to a halt outside the cell of a con named Curly.

An ex-Golden Gloves boxer, Curly was the meanest, roughest, most troublesome inmate in the prison. He'd caused the warden more problems than me, had spent more time in the Hole than me. His face and fists were festooned with scars. He was a legend, king of the joint. Once he had outfought seven cops armed with billy clubs. Black hair streaked with gray, he'd spent about twenty of his forty-two years in prison on a murder charge. Nobody, but nobody, messed with him.

"Can I talk to you, Curly?"

"I heard you got religion in the Hole," Curly said as I walked in, joining eight or nine other cons who were hanging around.

"That's right. This dude Jesus is so big that He has enough love for everybody, including you."

Laughter from the cons tumbled through the cell.

The guy laughing the loudest was the most obnoxious. He was a defrocked Catholic priest. Everybody still called him Father John. He'd lost his church years ago, so the story went, after he raped one of his parishioners, a 16-year-old girl. He'd been excommunicated and was doing remand time, awaiting trial on a charge of armed robbery.

Father John knew the Bible much better than I did.

"That Book," he spit out, "is the greatest sex novel ever written. You men ever read the story of Onan in Genesis? He had a real problem. Refused to consummate his marriage to Tamar. He spilled his seed on the ground. God killed him for being a pervert. Ever read about Lot's daughters who made out with their own father? Their own father, mind you. And David who ordered Bathsheba to shack up with him. And how about Solomon and his thousand wives and concubines? He had an orgy going for him every night. You guys want to read a groovy book, you read the Bible."

I was wondering how to answer him. He made the Bible sound pornographic, like it was all filthy sex. To me the Book was pure and clean and simple. It reflected the good and bad in men and women. But it was God, it was Jesus, and Father John had malignantly twisted it around.

"Shut your mouth!" Curly declared. "The next guy who razzes the Bible or Ruud I'll hit so hard that I'll knock his neck down to where his ankles are."

Everybody dummied up. The laughter was over.

"Ruud used to curse and swear," Curly went on. "Now he's carrying a Bible and talking about love. He's got something. Look at him, there's a shine on his face. He's talking about Jesus, not the next job he's going to pull on the outside. He's happier than any of us. Brian, you don't have to convince me there is a God. Just by looking at you, I know there is. How did it happen to you? Tell me."

"I read the Bible and then fell to my knees and prayed and then, man, I found it. Jesus came right out of these pages and gave me the coolest trip I've ever had. And Curly, the same thing can happen to you."

Without shame, in sight of everyone—a couple of guards had come up by now to listen in—Curly went to his knees. "Pray for me, Brian," he said.

I reached out and took him by the hand. "Jesus, you've got to let Curly know you are alive and you care for him. If you would have died for anyone, you would have done it just for him. Touch his life, Jesus, and change him into a new person like you did me."

I looked over at the prisoners standing by the cell door, and they were looking like, Ruud if this doesn't work, you are gonna be in big trouble; Curly better not be disappointed.

All of a sudden, Curly looked up from under the Bible I had

laid on his head and said, "Brian, I can see what it's all about. I know now what it is to experience Jesus and to feel his forgiveness. Thanks."

I said, "Don't thank me, Curly, just thank Jesus. He's the one who's done it all."

When the warden heard about it, he told the guard, "Hey, you better lock that Ruud up before he turns this place into a Bible school."

Later that week, a guy named Tommy, who had made fun of me while I preached in the bull pen, came by my cell. In a soft voice, he said, "I apologize. I'm sorry for the things I said. I let my bitterness overcome me. If I get out of here, I'm going to start again. I've been lost too long. Brian, tomorrow I go to court. Would you pray for me?" We knelt and prayed.

Tommy never came back to Prince Albert. The court ruled he was innocent. Curly transformed himself into a model prisoner, and we became the closest of friends as we studied the Bible together.

The next day I found six tabs of speed under my pillow, wrapped in a paper napkin.

Once I would have gulped them without a second thought, but my only reaction now was how they got there, who put them there. A while later, Alex Cordova was outside my cell. "Did you get the junk I left for you?"

I handed the speed back to Alex. "I don't need this junk anymore. I've found a natural high."

"I guess you're playing it cool," he said. "You always were a terrific con man. This religious scam I've heard you're on is a sensational gimmick. It's going to sound great to the judge. Probably reduce your sentence."

I beheld Alex now as someone I had known in another life. There was a glaze to his eyes, indicating he was tripping out. I couldn't imagine what I'd once found so hypnotically appealing about him.

"Alex, it's not a scam. Coming to Jesus is the biggest high I've ever had. I'm not getting off this trip—ever."

"Sure, sure, kid, but you can level with your old buddy."

I thought of all the hits we'd made together, all the parties
. . . and the lingering ache in my side.

"Alex, I want you to know that I forgive you."

"What are you talking about?"

"I forgive you for stabbing me. It wasn't you, but drugs that
sent that blade into me. Alex, I'd like to talk to you about Christ."

"Save it for the suckers," he said. "You can't hustle a hustler."

"I'd like to hustle you into heaven."

"Are you for real?" he said incredulously.

"Yes, and so is Jesus."

"Okay, okay. You keep your scam running. Religion is a
good racket. It's a great way to steal legally."

Before I could plead further with him, Alex walked off and
walked out of my life. The only regret I had concerning him was
that I hadn't been able to bring him to the Lord.

November 27, 1965

Dear Mom and Dad,

First of all, please sit down because you won't be able
to take my news standing up.

I asked for a Bible while I was in the Hole and,
praise the Lord, Jesus came to me.

God is closer to me than the ground.

He is in my heart for keeps, and you'd better believe
it. Hallelujah! I've read all the gospels, and they're
beautiful.

I've learned all the names of the books of the Bible by
heart and memorized a lot of verses. I don't know
which verses to memorize, so when you write send me
some suggestions.

Dad, I didn't know life could be so great, even in
jail. God has given me a dream of praying for a great
multitude, and I know it will come true.

Oh, Dad, I could say so much more, but I'm not
allowed to write on the back of this piece of paper.

I'm leaving the charges against me up to God. Even

141

if I get thirty years, I'll serve God in jail. All I can say is someday you and I are going to walk those golden streets together hand in hand with the Lord.

You were right all along. Pray for me, and then you'll know what I'm writing is true.

Lots of love.

Your son,

Brian.

P.S. They're calling me "Reverend" in here. Write soon, Dad, and let everybody read this letter. I want everybody to know.

Hallelujah!

Please send me a new Bible.

December 4, 1965

Dear Mom and Dad,

I sure praise and thank the Lord for saving my soul and keeping me close to Him. I know I'll never go back to sin.

I'm reading the Book of Acts and Romans, and I've memorized a few more verses. Isn't it great knowing that there's a lot more power in reading the Bible than most people think? Praise the Lord.

Mom, I haven't smoked since I was saved. The Devil has tried to get me to smoke, but I just had to show him that Jesus was in my heart and he couldn't push Him around.

I got your letter, Dad, and thanks for the Bible.

Mom, Dad, coming to jail this time was the greatest thing that ever happened in my life because it led me to the Lord. Just think—if I hadn't come to jail maybe I would never have known God.

Boy, I sure would like to be outside and prove to you and everybody else how I've changed.

Tell Donna, Dave, and Faithe I'm praying for them.

I've gained more than twenty pounds. Been eating like a maniac since I got out of the Hole. I trade my cigarette and tobacco ration for extra food. I even got a haircut. And all the pimples the doctor said would never leave my face are gone. I'm doing push-ups and every kind of exercise possible to build my strength.

And God has given me a whole new mind, too. I can think clearly and logically.

Everybody is still calling me "Reverend."

Dad, I hate to ask, but can you get a lawyer for me and go my bail? I'd like to be home for Christmas.

It's up to you. No hard feelings if you don't get me out.

Oh God, my whole life has been such a disgrace to the Lord. I know it's hard for you to believe I'm changed. But I am.

Write soon

Lots of love,

Brian.

P.S. I tell everyone here what I believe and so far most of them are listening.

December 11, 1965

Dear Mom and Dad,

Dad, you should have sent more paper. I filled the whole notebook you did send with my first message and testimony and I would like to rewrite it and start on another message. Don't worry about me. I'm fighting the Devil every day and standing for Jesus.

Mom, if you think you're happy about my being saved, imagine how happy I am.

I've got a lot of plans, Dad, to serve God whether I stay in jail or get out. I want to give my whole life to

God. Remember that evangelist in Winnipeg who said I was to become a preacher? He was right. I only pray that God will humble me enough and make me worthy to serve Him as an evangelist.

I'm in Revelation now. I have a few chapters left. I will have started the whole Bible from the beginning and will be reading Genesis by the time you receive this letter.

Dad, I thank God for what He is doing. I'm sure He is going to do a lot more. Hallelujah and praise Jesus.

Write soon.

Lots of love,

Reverend Brian Douglas Ruud

Mom looked young as a teen-ager and Dad beamed as I related step by step the account of the new wine that had been poured into the new bottle that was their son.

We were talking in the visitors' room. Dad put his arm around Mom, both choking back sobs.

Mom said: "This can't be my son."

"Yes, this is our son," Dad said. "This is the new Brian. Jesus has brought him back to us."

My folks had applied for and received permission for a special midweek visit, which was only supposed to last twenty minutes. But we talked and had prayer and praised God for hours. We made such joyful noises to the Lord that the guards didn't know what to think. So they locked us in, and we stayed all afternoon.

In the course of the conversation, Mom said that she had prayed the hardest she had ever prayed one particular night not long ago. Figuring the time of her prayer carefully, I deduced that she was talking to God at those precise moments when I had tried twice—and twice failed—to scale the ladder to get to the drugs in the attic of the garage. If I had made it up the ladder, the police would have found drugs on my person.

After I wrote my first letter to Dad with the exciting news that I'd been saved, I'd sweated it out, waiting for him to answer.

It took over a week for him to write back. He explained that he and Mom had been out of town. When they'd come home and Dad saw my letter, he thought it was just another routine note asking for something or other. Mom was so ill and worried about me he wasn't going to read her the letter. But God told him to open that envelope. When he and Mom did read it, they were speechless with joy and thanked merciful Jesus for my deliverance.

"Now," said Mom as they left, "you're the son I've always prayed you would be."

"The prodigal has come home," my father added.

Dad had told me that he was going to preach about "the most miraculous conversion experience I've ever heard of" at his next service. The result was a flood of gifts to me from his parishoners —nuts, chocolates, candy, and cakes.

I gave it all away as Christmas presents to other cons and because Jesus had moved inside me again, promising that I would make it home for His birthday.

"Brian," Curly said, "you'd better keep some of these things for yourself, just in case it doesn't work out."

"'No, man, I know Jesus is going to let me spend Christmas with my family."

Friday rolled around, the last day before the holiday began. Dad had said he would try to raise my bail. If it didn't come through today, I'd spend Christmas in jail. But the morning and most of the afternoon had already vanished without word. The clock traveled to 4:45. Another fifteen minutes and the entire courthouse apparatus would be closed until the holiday ended.

"Get your street clothes on," a guard told me at 4:55. "You're out on bail."

"Hey, Ruud, you gotta pray one more time before you go," one con shouted.

I looked at the guard and he nodded yes.

"Jesus, I hope you'll help all my friends here to understand how beautiful you are, and that what really matters is what we've got on the inside. Jesus, make them happy like you've made me happy. Turn them on real good. Help them to know you, Lord, help them to find you, Lord. Amen."

Then a con continued the prayer: "Jesus," he said, awkwardly, "please bring Brian back to us just as soon as you can."

Unquestionably, that prayer would be answered.

"It's a miracle," Dad said as we were driving home. "I phoned everyone I knew to try and raise your bail. It just seemed that no one had the money. Then I went to the bank. The manager told me he'd read about you and that you were a bad risk. He said that in any case he couldn't consider the loan until after Christmas. He'd need the approval of his board. I told him I'd be back after lunch and that I knew the money would be waiting. He said I'd be wasting my time. But he was waiting for me when I returned. The strangest thing had happened, he said. After I left, his board members had all come into the bank, though none of them were scheduled to be there. They approved the loan and said it was unprecedented, that they'd never done anything like it before."

We spent Christmas day in Victoria with Donna and her husband—the most joyous, relaxed Christmas I'd ever had, the first time I'd celebrated His birthday with the proper spirit, with goodwill to all men.

Christmas night some kids who lived a few doors from my sister invited me to a party. The atmosphere was all too familiar —drugs, booze, smoking, sex.

I politely excused myself and left five minutes after arrival, but not before reminding them they were doing a dreadful job of celebrating the Savior's nativity. They were too tripped out to know what I was talking about. When we returned home, I refused invitations to dozens of holiday parties. I told my friends I was into a new scene and wouldn't come unless I could preach about Jesus. The invitations were quickly withdrawn.

"I love Jesus" were the first words of the first sermon I ever delivered in a church. I never got to say more than that. All I could do was cry. The Spirit of God swept through the church like a flood, and, even though they couldn't understand all my words, they knew something had changed Brian Ruud.

For the service the following week, Dad put an ad in the *Star*

146

Phoenix announcing that I would minister and give my testimony. I didn't think there would be much of a crowd. Because of me, my Dad's congregation had been running low for years.

When we reached the church we found it packed. Extra chairs had to be brought from the basement.

"I know you've all come to hear my son speak," Dad said from the pulpit after the singing.

I was sitting in the back row with Mom. "I'm scared. I can't go through with it. I can't admit what I've been in front of all these people. They won't believe I'm transformed."

"Yes, they will," she answered firmly. "And, anyway, you won't be preaching." When I stared at her in perplexity she added: "It will be Jesus speaking, using you as His vessel."

"It's all yours, Brian," I heard Dad announce.

I went to the pulpit, still feeling nervous and guilty.

Then a love—like a bower of sunshine—settled in me and the same love came down and settled in the church.

I spoke for more than an hour, gaining more confidence with every sentence. The sermon was a victory for Him.

Afterwards, Dad said, "Brian, if I died right now, I'd feel my life is complete. Tonight I saw the son I've been yearning to see for many years."

"The Lord has already done more for me than I dared hope," said Mom, coming to me and kissing me. "Brian, never stop serving Jesus."

I preached regularly after that. In addition to telling the story of my life and rebirth, I repeatedly emphasized that with Jesus no one need fear the future.

"On behalf of Her Majesty the Queen against Brian Douglas Ruud." Those formidable words opened my trial.

"Stand to your feet and take the prisoner's box," the judge told me.

As I obeyed his order, I silently summoned a Bible passage I'd committed to memory. For the ordeal I was facing I needed the strength from Luke 12:11–12, "And when they bring you unto . . . magistrates, and powers, take ye no thought how or

147

what thing ye shall answer, or what ye shall say: For the Holy Ghost shall teach you in the same hour what ye ought to say."

At least I had never faced this judge and prosecutor before, although I was certain they both were aware of my record.

The prosecutor's first move was a surprise. To save the Crown time and expense, the prosecution had decided to drop two of the charges, that of possession of stolen property and breaking and entering with intent. They felt they would use the same evidence to convict me on the last, most drastic charge against me—possession of drugs and narcotics.

The judge went over what had happened at my three preliminary hearings, and then replied, "Does the defendant understand the remaining charge against him?"

"Yes, your Honor."

"Where is your attorney?"

"I can't afford one."

The judge asked the prosecutor, "Who is on the docket who can represent Mr. Ruud?"

The prosecutor read a list of names. When he was finished, I said, "Your Honor, I don't want a lawyer."

"You will not be billed for this. When an individual cannot afford an attorney the Crown will appoint one and pay for it."

"I understand that. But I *do* have a lawyer."

"I'm not sure I follow you," he said with exasperation. "First you said you didn't want an attorney and now you claim you have one. If you are represented, where is your attorney? Why isn't he here?"

"Your Honor, it's like this. When I was in jail, I gave my heart to Jesus Christ. I gave Him my life. He delivered me and helped me and I've been praying. I know He is in this courtroom, helping to represent me."

The judge sputtered and called a recess.

One of the officers—the term *bull* was no longer part of my vocabulary—who'd busted me came over and said, "They're going to cook you, Ruud. The remaining charge of drug possession is very, very serious. You're going to be off the streets for a long time. You're going to need more than Jesus to walk out of here a free man."

148

But I didn't look at it that way. I said to myself, *Thank you, Jesus. Two down. One to go.*

When the court was reconvened, the judge said, "If you wish, Mr. Ruud, you may act as your own counsel."

"Thank you, your Honor."

"How do you plead?"

"Not guilty."

I pled not guilty and would do my best to obtain an acquittal because I didn't feel in my heart that Jesus wanted me to be convicted. A stranger named Brian Ruud had committed the pharmacy caper. The new Brian Ruud wouldn't steal a paper clip.

The prosecutor called policeman after policeman, all of whom placed me in the garage among the stolen drugs.

When I cross-examined them, they all admitted, however, that they had not found drugs on my body or in my clothes. (*Thank you, Mom. Thank you, Jesus.*)

Several lawyers and a number of university law students were in the courtroom listening to me conduct my own defense. They'd turned out, I supposed, because of the curious situation of an untrained 19-year-old going up against all the power of Her Majesty the Queen.

I had noted several times that the prosecutor had referred to me as "my learned friend." That was pretty cool. I liked the sound of it. I thought I'd return the courtesy, but the first time I called *him* "my learned friend" he shot up and declared, "I am not *your* learned friend."

The spectators, including my folks and a lot of people from our church, howled with laughter. Then the judge admonished the prosecutor for being impolite. "If *he* is your learned friend, then you must be *his* learned friend," his Honor said.

The trial was running to a swift conclusion—and I was a goner. The picture that had been painted of me by the police made me sound terrible, and there was little I could do on my own behalf. I knew I was going to be found guilty and the only question in my mind was how heavy the sentence would be.

To assure a conviction, the prosecutor called a final witness who would confound everyone in the court. His testimony would not be what the prosecutor expected to hear, or what I expected to hear.

He was a middle-aged dude in a wrinkled suit who identified himself as a police laboratory technical expert. He'd been flown in from Regina to testify. The loot that had been recovered from my caper at the pharmacy was stacked on a large table at one side of the courtroom. The prosecutor showed the lab man a bottle, which I remembered handling. I knew my prints were all over it.

"Have you examined this bottle for fingerprints?" the prosecutor asked.

"Yes."

"Are the fingerprints of the accused on this bottle?"

I glanced over at Dad, my heart beating so loud I thought everyone could hear it. Well, I thought, if God wants me back in jail, I'm ready and willing to face it. But the lab man hesitated before answering.

"Are they the prints of the accused or not?" the judge demanded impatiently.

"Well . . . at first I thought they were. I reported that tentative conclusion to the Crown prosecutor. Then I made several more tests, and changed my opinion. Something . . . something . . . had happened to the prints."

"Happened?" the prosecutor said with astonishment.

"Yes. I'm afraid I cannot absolutely say the prints on the bottle match the prints of the accused."

A cheer went up from the spectators' section. The judge called for order and said he'd clear the room if there was another outburst.

"Are you certain?" the judge asked.

"Yes, your Honor. Prints taken from a hard, smooth surface like glass are easy to test. There's no mistaking the fact that the two sets of prints are not identical."

The judge jumped to his feet. "Are you actually saying that the prints don't match?"

"That's right, your Honor. The prints do not match, and I cannot testify otherwise."

I held my breath, as amazed as everyone else.

The flustered prosecutor next showed the lab expert two glass tubes. He said: "One of these tubes contains hair found entangled in the screen of the pharmacy where the crime was committed. And it also contains hair removed from the pillowcase owned by the accused. This second tube contains a sample of hair from the head of the accused."

Now the prosecutor asked the witness, "Have you examined both samples of hair?"

"Yes, I have. In great detail."

"Do they match?"

"They are of the same texture. Both samples are blond and curly. Both have been dipped in every chemical solution we have, given every test. The two samples of hair are similar, but not exact."

"Is it the same hair?" the judge interposed.

"The samples appear to be the same, but I cannot say with certitude that they are the same, that they came from the same head."

The courtroom broke into pandemonium. I was too numb and dazed to react. So was the judge, who pounded his gavel for order, then declared: "The case against the accused is dismissed. The accused is acquitted."

That night in bed I thought how superpowerful was my friend from the shores of Galilee, how all things *were* possible once you gave yourself to the super-cool soul Man. Far into the night my mind roamed as I searched for the answer as to why He had performed the miraculous transformation of the evidence against me.

Again I realized that it was the old Brian Ruud who had committed that caper. Jesus was showing mercy to the new Brian Ruud. But there had to be more to it than mercy.

The answer finally came! I had been granted the miracle of the nonmatching fingerprints and hair *so that I could preach for Him and do His work. And because I was no longer the commandment killer.*

I opened my Bible and read John 14:21:

> He that hath my commandments, and keepeth them,
> he it is that loveth me; and he that loveth me shall
> be loved of my Father, and I will love him, and will
> manifest myself to him.

13

Rugged Cross, Rugged Days

Ye have heard that it hath been said, Thou shalt love thy neighbour, and hate thine enemy.

But I say unto you, Love your enemies, bless them that curse you, do good to them that hate you, and pray for them which despitefully use you, and persecute you.

MATTHEW 5:43–44

So long as I remained steadfast to Jesus, there was no prison big enough to hold me, no court big enough to convict me.

Jesus was my rock, sword, and shield, watching over and protecting me as I moved into full-time evangelism with the approach of my twentieth birthday.

I was to learn quickly that there would be triumphs in serving Him, but there would also be defeats, humiliations, and disappointments. It would take grit, tenacity, dedication, turning on

153

to Him every waking moment. It would take white, pure faith before the multitudes would come, before the breakthrough that would enable me to pass on to throngs what had been so majestically given to me, pass on to sin-shackled teen-agers and adults the way, the truth, and the life through commitment to Christ.

The plague that was the Devil, more than any time in history, was running wild, loose, and victorious in the world. It seemed more men cleaved to Satan than to God. That this was so struck me as a horrible paradox. Christ demanded so little in exchange for how much He gave. I knew that if He could change me so drastically, He could change anyone. I therefore pledged myself body and soul, nonstop and tirelessly, to breaching the palisades of sin erected by the Devil. Without doubt, that was why Jesus had bestowed salvation on me, freed me from prison and entrusted me with the same great commission that He gave his disciples in Mark 16:15, "Go ye into all the world, and preach the gospel to every creature."

There were unsaved creatures aplenty on the West Side. One evening after giving my sermon in Dad's church, I decided to go to the legger's and preach deliverance to what Christ described in Luke 4:18 as the brokenhearted, the captives, the blind, "to set at liberty them that are bruised."

As usual, it was jammed with dudes and chicks high on drugs and booze. The sarcasm and insults pricked like thorns.

"Here's the holy preacher!"

"We've missed you, Brian. Aren't we good enough for you anymore?"

"Hey, let's have a ball, let's turn the preacher on."

A dude offered me a drink, and when I refused, he offered me speed.

"No, man, I don't need them now."

"Sure you do," he said, the words rolling like polluted water over the spittle-drenched sea of his black beard. "You just need a little persuasion."

"I love you and I've come to tell you how wonderful Jesus is."

"You're going to turn on whether you want to or not."

Several of them grabbed me, threw me to the floor, and began rinsing my hair and face from a bottle of flowing whiskey. They were trying to force my mouth open to drink the booze and drop the pills. Lord, I thought, why would you allow this to happen? I only came here to tell them about what you did for me, and now they're trying to get me back on drugs. But then I remembered I was supposed to be a follower of Jesus. I had led the way instead of letting Jesus lead me. I had really asked for trouble. Oh God, please help me out of this, and from now on I'll only go where you lead.

The shouting, cursing, and laughter died. Everyone's gaze was riveted on the entrance. Standing there was an avenging angel in the person of a scar-faced brontosaurus I hadn't seen since prison.

"Brian, what are you doing on the floor?" Curly asked in a voice gentle, yet potentially murderous. "Why doesn't somebody help him?" said the man who was my first convert.

"Curly, am I glad to see you," I said.

"Nobody trying to hurt you, are they?" Curly asked.

No one dared tangle with Curly. He had sized up the scene in an instant, but instead of wading in and throwing punches he acted with commanding, confident restraint, which I found remarkable. The old Curly would have hit first, asked questions afterwards.

"No, it's all right," I said, getting up. "Let's split."

I introduced my folks to Curly, and told them how he had rescued me. Curly stayed with us, and he and I spent hour after hour reminiscing. He said that shortly after his conversion Christ had put everything together for him as He had for me. He'd been unexpectedly released several months ahead of schedule! The warden had told him he was rehabilitated. "The warden was right," Curly said with a grin. "But it was Jesus, not the prison, that did the rehabilitating."

We talked about the Lord, and Curly said he was into the Bible, reading it constantly. But he remained tight-lipped about his future plans. I wanted him to stay with us permanently, help out at the church, and join me in revivals as soon as I was ready to travel.

155

A few days later, without leaving a note or saying good-bye, Curly vanished. I tried for weeks without success to locate him.

To this day I keep Curly in my prayers, and know our paths are going to cross again, if not in this life then in heaven.

By summer Dad was lining up tent meetings, and he asked me to preach at his week-long revival in Birch Hills, a small farming community about 140 miles from Saskatoon.

I blitzed the town with tracts and invitations to the revival, going door-to-door and in front of bars and pool halls. The revival went extremely well, dozens responding to the call to let Jesus into their hearts.

The final day of the meeting was to be on Sunday, but Dad said he had to be back in Saskatoon for his church service. He told me to close out the revival alone.

More than one hundred people gathered as I got up to preach my message—"How the Prodigal Son Came Home." Two dudes, obviously drunk, began acting up in the back, completely destroying the holy mood under God's canvas. Their blasphemies drowned me out.

I closed my eyes, bowed my head, and prayed. "Dear Jesus, these men are no worse than I was and I know you love them as you love me. Lord, what they need is a little bit of you. I ask that you forgive them for breaking up your service, for coming to church drunk, and that right now, Lord, they'll receive your love, and that you'll save them."

When I opened my eyes both men were kneeling in front of me.

One said he had been saved years before but had backslid. Both apologized for their behavior and gave themselves to Jesus as I laid hands on them and prayed them on through to Christ. The revival had ended in glory.

The June night was warm and a fresh breeze rustled in from the river as I arrived back in Saskatoon at about twelve-thirty A.M. I dropped our microphone equipment and several boxes of hymn books at the church and headed toward home.

At the intersection of Seventh Avenue and Windsor Street, the car began chugging. I was out of gas. In a moment, a car pulled up next to mine. Its occupants seemed familiar, and one looked like a policeman I knew.

"I just ran out of gas," I said, hoping they'd give me a lift to an all-night service station. Instead they roared off without a word.

I pushed the car against the curb, locked the doors, opened the trunk, and removed my Honda motor scooter. I'd pick up a gallon of gas myself.

As I started to kick the Honda into movement, three police cars swooped up, doors flaring open. I recognized all seven of the policemen who were coming toward me. My first thought was that this was ridiculous overkill—my car wasn't stolen, I'd given the police no trouble for months, I wasn't breaking any law. Why were they out in such force?

The seven of them formed a ring around me. One cop overturned my Honda and stomped on it. A big, stocky officer with a black crew cut who must have weighed 250 pounds spit at my feet. "I hear you're preaching now, Ruud."

"That's right."

"Do you remember the time about a year ago when I was going to search you in that cafe on the West Side on suspicion of concealing drugs? A couple of your pals came in and threatened me. Well, the odds have changed now, haven't they?"

"I don't know what you're talking about. I don't remember the incident, although it may have happened. I did those kind of things then. But since Jesus Christ came into my life, I'm different. I spend all my time trying to help people as much as I can."

Another officer said, "We hear you pulled a few tricks in your last court case. Who did you pay off to get those fingerprints and hair changed?"

"No one. It was a miracle that Jesus gave me."

"We don't believe in miracles," a third officer said. "Level with us. This religious kick of yours is just a money-making gaff. You're in it to con people, aren't you?"

"No. I'm one hundred percent serious about my work for Jesus."

"You're a phony," the crew-cut cop said. "Come on, let's get him."

The circle tightened and they began shoving me from man to

157

man. Somebody ripped my jacket. Then another car screeched up and, my God, there were now nine policemen pushing, kicking, tripping, and tossing me around like a Ping-Pong ball. I'd already smelled liquor on them.

This was not the time to be a hero. But I couldn't see a way out. I didn't mind a working over too much, but their mood was so ugly that I was afraid I'd end up like one of the stiffs—suicides, murder victims, winos—whose bloated bodies were frequently washed ashore on the banks of the river.

"Let's finish him," said the giant with the crew cut. He seemed the leader and the most vindictive. If they killed me, there would be nine of them implicated and it would be difficult to keep it a secret. But that was small consolation as one of them put his hands around my neck and applied so much pressure I could scarcely breathe.

I called on Jesus: *Did you save me so that I would end up a revenge victim of nine drunken cops? But if that's your will, I'm ready to go.*

Try, Brian, try. I was sure that was Jesus speaking to me.

All of a sudden I felt a power come upon me that I knew was the anointing spirit of God. I jumped up, knocking the cop off balance, and he fell backward. Then I went into a spin, gaining momentum, and crashed through the circle like a fullback finding daylight.

I ran down the street and quickly jumped over a fence, all the cops in hot pursuit. I found a bike on the lawn of a house and pedaled furiously through an empty lot, past a Catholic church and into an alley. Gradually, my pulse and heart stopped racing.

After an hour, I thought it was safe to return to my car.

When I got there I transferred from the bike to my overturned Honda. I planned to make it home as quickly as possible and pick up the car the next day. I looked up and all of a sudden, one of the patrol cars barrelled around the corner, fishtailing on the gravel, and headed straight toward me. They'd been waiting and apparently wanted to try a second time to kill me. I shouted "Jesus" and at the same time, dived through the air, throwing myself clear of the bike. The car hit the bike, smashing it into pieces.

I picked myself up and ran again, this time to a nearby school, hurling myself over another fence and hiding behind a large clump of bushes. I waited.

Two of the cops soon were searching the grounds. Then another one joined them. The trio was so close to me I could overhear their conversation.

"Hey, Joe, any sight of Ruud?" one cop asked the latest arrival.

"No," Joe answered, "I thought I saw him on the other side of the schoolyard a few moments ago. Strangest thing, though. It wasn't Ruud, but it was *someone*. *Someone* who had, well, a kind of glow about him. But when I got there he disappeared."

Finally they left and I made it home on foot by four A.M. When I reached our porch I saw the door was open. That was unusual. Was our house being burglarized, or were the cops waiting inside for me?

As soon as I stepped in I understood. Dad had left the door ajar for me. He was on his knees in the front room, praying, "Jesus, where is my son? Since he's been saved he's never been out this late. Please watch over him. Lord, wherever he is send your angels to protect him and bring him home safely to us."

"Dad," I said quietly. "Thank you. I'm sure your prayers saved my life."

I told him what had happened. "Dad, who do you suppose that one policeman saw on the school grounds?"

"We'll have to ask Jesus about that when we see Him."

Dad phoned the station house and a sergeant was at our home in ten minutes. I told him the entire story too, identified all my attackers, not expecting another cop to believe me. But he drove us in his car to where the assault had taken place. I showed him the bike and my damaged, overturned motor scooter. A police van arrived and photographs were taken of the bike and the scooter. Everything was dusted for fingerprints.

It was close to eight A.M. when we got to the station. The sergeant phoned the chief of police and he, the sergeant said, was going to phone the mayor. The story, if it became public knowledge, would scandalize the Saskatoon police department.

To their credit, none of the higher officials of the city or the police department exerted any pressure on me. They did not apologize for the officers or try to talk me out of filing charges.

In a few weeks, the investigation was completed. The chief of police invited me to his office to sign the complaint. I had talked it over with Dad, who said it was necessary that my attackers be punished. He wasn't antipolice, nor was I. But there were bad cops as there were bad preachers.

When I reached the chief's office, he put the complaint before me, his manner polite but grim. Lord, I wondered, is this what you want me to do? If I sign, those cops will lose their jobs. Their careers will be over. And their families will suffer as well. I held the pen in my hand, undecided.

Jesus, I thought, if you were in this predicament I know what you would do. You would show compassion and mercy and love. That's what you're all about.

Brian, Jesus answered, *they murdered me and I didn't lift a hand. I forgave them. Let me fight your battles.*

"Sir," I said to the chief, "I've changed my mind. I'm not going to sign. Let's forget about it. Just tell those officers that I'm sorry they don't like me. In a way, I can't blame them. But I have no desire to see them suffer anymore than I'm sure they've already suffered."

The chief's face showed delight and relief. "Are you sure, Mr. Ruud, this is what you want to do?"

"Yes."

He shook my hand and wished me luck. "I'm going to ask the men to come and hear you preach. I think they can learn a great deal from you."

"They're all welcome."

A few nights later several of the policemen who'd been involved in the incident were in our church with their wives. None of them answered my altar call, but after hearing me preach I hoped they went home convinced that I was a new man in Christ.

A few weeks after that I became convinced that there was no lingering enmity between the police department and myself. I was hurrying along Avenue P one evening when I was flagged down for speeding.

The policeman was young, maybe a few years older than me. I'd never seen him before. Probably new on the force.

Gruffly, he asked for my license. I gave it to him and as he examined it the look of belligerence on his face changed.

"You're Brian Ruud?"

"Yes sir."

"The preacher?"

"That's right. As a matter of fact, I'm supposed to start preaching in less than ten minutes. I've been visiting and praying with one of my Dad's sick parishioners on the other side of town. I stayed too long and I'm late. That's why I was speeding."

I made it to church on time thanks to the officer. Siren blazing, I had a police escort all the way. I walked to the pulpit, smiling.

What had interested me most about the entire episode, what had been most significant in the lopsided attack, was the person that policeman had seen on the school grounds, that *someone* who disappeared.

It wasn't much of a mystery. The one who had been there had not only protected me, but kept me from signing the complaint that would have ruined the careers of all the policemen involved.

Perhaps each of those officers now believed in miracles.

14

Walkin' With the Man

*The young lions do lack, and
suffer hunger: but they that seek
the Lord shall not want any good
thing.*

PSALMS 34:10

In my new star bright world there was both peace
and war. Peace came from fully embracing the dictum in Matthew 22:37, "Thou shalt love the Lord thy God with all thy
heart, and with all thy soul, and with all thy mind." But inside me
raged the frustration of finding my way as an evangelist so that I
could spread His gospel everywhere. Despite the paucity of my
education, I had mastered—from my own bittersweet experience
—the weapon with which every abomination of the Devil could
be conquered. I had the answer to all the problems torturing
mankind and since I had been called by Jesus to preach, I
yearned to be—as soon as possible—a soaringly effective young
lion for the Lord.

But even a young lion had to grow and learn how to hunt.

The drug scene had reached epidemic proportions in Canada

and the United States. Sin in a thousand other guises punished the souls of millions of young people and adults. To fight Satan, to win souls, I became convinced a new hammer and anvil were necessary, an approach that ignored the labels of denominationalism, which had largely turned me off. It didn't matter which church people chose to attend. The church as such was often a creaky structure, over-organized, concerned with trivia and constructing buildings that were too often empty or half-filled. As a body, the church had failed for the most part—primarily because it lacked the spirit and ardor of evangelism, because it didn't preach the real Christ I knew, the Christ of miracles and abundance.

I wanted to preach before multitudes, tell the world how a dude like me had had his pact with the Devil cancelled for a contract, forever unbreakable, with Christ. I didn't care if my congregations were Pentecostals, Methodists, Baptists, Catholics, Jews, or atheists. After coming to Christ, getting excited about Him, the converts could worship in any building they chose. Then they could continue to serve Him by turning on their own churches to the living, genuine Christ. The all-important precondition for heaven in this life, for heaven everlasting, was embracing Jesus. After taking that vaulting step, everything else would fall in place.

And so I concluded that the only "denomination" that mattered was "Jesus-ism."

I had a special burden of compassion for teen-agers who had tuned out the church. Their trouble, as mine had been, wasn't so much that they were unchurched. Their trouble was that they were not Jesus people.

I realized, too, that there were many good things about the church and organized religion. The buildings, after all, were necessary, but I wanted to see those buildings overflowing with people going foursquare down the line for Jesus. I had read with considerable interest in both the secular press and religious publications that the two fastest growing denominations in Canada and the States were the Pentecostals and the Baptists, both fundamental and evangelical. Also a whole new group of independent churches had sprung up, where Christ was taught as Christ should be taught.

These were the churches and the approach that were meeting the needs of those mired in sin, people spinning out their lives without direction and commitment, people who did not know the truth of Jeremiah 30:17—"I will heal thee of thy wounds, saith the Lord."

Before I could even dream of putting my own ideas into force and build a meaningful ministry of my own, I knew that there was an apprenticeship to be served, a time of testing.

As a young lion in Christ, I began to hunt souls wherever people would listen, wherever they would not listen. I was to founder before finding my direction. I was to learn that the gospel trail would be no easier for me than it had been for Paul. I was to discover that often the only thing that would keep me going was faith forged of iron.

Above all, I felt the Lord was leading me to a different type of ministry, not quite like that of any other evangelist.

Visiting Donna in Victoria, I began giving my testimony in small churches. After I'd preached, one pastor told me, "Your message is wonderful. But what you have to do now is go to Bible school for four years and get some of those rough edges smoothed out."

But I didn't see it that way, and neither had Christ when He came to me and beckoned me to preach. He had made it clear that if He wanted a seminary graduate to hurl His thunderbolts at a dying world, He wouldn't have chosen me.

Anyway, I wasn't sure how many rough edges I had. I may have mispronounced a word here and there, but I was improving my vocabulary through self-study, speaking now in an argot that both kids and adults understood. I wasn't the world's greatest preacher, but experience was honing my style and people seemed to respond. Also I knew the Bible and I knew Jesus. Perhaps my rough edges cut through the veils of sin better than smooth ones.

I was introduced to Reverend Curtis Mitchell, a heavyset pastor with glasses, who had the same feeling for Christ as I did. He had

165

a church in Surrey, a suburb of Vancouver, and a Skid Row mission in the downtown area of the city. Pastor Mitchell invited me to stay in his home, work with the young people in his church, preach at his mission, and join him in radio rallies.

I grooved on the work, but it lasted only a short time. Reverend Mitchell's expenses were heavy, his offerings barely meeting his needs. He couldn't afford to provide me even with living expenses, which is all I wanted in exchange for the opportunity to grow in the Lord's work. Before I left, he bought me a new suit and told me to put myself in the hands of God.

The easiest course would have been to tag along behind my Dad, working with him in his church and at his revivals. But he had labored most of his life to build his ministry, and I didn't want to intrude. In addition, I had a burning compulsion to move out on my own.

In taking Pastor Mitchell's advice to put myself in God's hands, I was directed toward my sister Faithe, who was living in Calgary, a city of almost a hundred thousand in southern Alberta, founded as a fort by the Mounties in 1875.

Blonde, pretty, bright-eyed, Faithe was also deep into the Jesus scene. At Christian Center Church, she played the organ, sang beautifully and was a real inspiration to other young people in the church. She also managed to hold down a full-time job as an executive secretary. Faithe and I had never seen eye to eye on much of anything until my conversion. But now we could communicate, now we had a common interest.

Faithe was well named. On faith alone she decided to step out with me on our cruise for Christ, leaving her comfortable way of life for what would surely be a perilous journey for Jesus. While Faithe was winding up her affairs, I preached at several churches in Calgary.

One day I received a phone call from a lady who'd heard my testimony. She asked me to her home to talk, she said, about the Lord.

When I arrived, there was another woman with her. Both were middle-aged and angry. I was no sooner in the door when they began berating me. One of the women said, "How dare you take out one of the girls in the Church? You're nothing but a punk and a gangster and a rapist. You have no right to stand in a holy pulpit and preach the Word of God."

I walked out, saying nothing, not understanding how such churchgoers could call themselves Christians, how such people could claim Jesus was in their hearts and yet ignore His teachings of forgiveness, compassion—His divine ability to restructure a life as admittedly dreadful as mine had once been. I was so depressed that I wondered if those women were correct. Did I have the right to preach?

The pain of that encounter stayed with me several days, and Satan came back to haunt me. I was in Faithe's apartment trying to type a sermon when I felt a craving in my body, and aching vibrations, migraine-strong, thrashed through my head. Since I'd been saved, I had not had the slightest urge for a tab of speed. Now that urge was so powerful I thought I couldn't resist.

Faithe walked in and I leveled with her about the consuming need for a trip that had welled in me.

"Fight it, Brian," she said. "Get hold of yourself. Shake the Devil. I know you can do it."

I prayed and thought of the dire consequences of reverting to drugs. Then I went to the Bible and John 14:13, "Whatsoever ye shall ask in my name, that will I do." I asked to be freed of the desire for drugs . . . and a moment later *I had freedom!* Since that experience I have never again craved drugs or even had a headache.

Fingers flying over the typewriter, I finished my sermon, one of the most powerful I've ever written. I titled it: "The Power of Prayer and Faith."

A few days before we were scheduled to leave Calgary, I was on my knees in the apartment, asking for two hundred dollars so that we could begin our travels for Jesus. As I prayed, a man I'd never seen before (presumably, he'd heard me preach) came in, walked to the couch and placed on the leatherette surface two fifty-dollar bills and five twenties. Then he silently left.

167

Again I learned how incredible and wonderful was the truth of John 14:13. I had asked in His name, and it had been given to me. Jesus worked in strange and mysterious ways, and He was a God who never failed.

Faithe and I left without a single scheduled revival or a single invitation to preach at a church. We were driving a battered, patch-tired, 8-year-old station wagon, which got us as far as Kansas City, Missouri. We arrived with eighteen dollars and no prospects or friends except Jesus.

I went to Calvary Temple and met the pastor, who agreed to let me preach at his church.

The meeting proved a rousing success. By the last night we had more than twelve hundred in attendance with chairs set up in the aisles for the unexpectedly large turnout. God delivered scores of people, healing them physically and mentally as they renounced drugs, booze, and cigarettes. I had never seen the Spirit move so effectively among so many, had never seen the will of the Lord so manifest. It was by far the largest meeting in which I had participated. Evidently, I had something to say that touched a chord in a great many hearts. Perhaps Jesus had not made an idle or frivolous choice in commanding me to preach in His name.

Next I was invited to bring revival to an all-Negro Assembly of God church in the ghetto of East St. Louis, Illinois. We stayed with Reverend Sylvester Haynes and his family. Pastor Haynes had purchased an old house that he was remodeling into a home for senior citizens of his congregation. I helped him out in the daytime, feeling a special delight in working as a carpenter, the same trade as Jesus.

To bring people to church, Faithe and I bustled through the surrounding area in the early evenings passing out tracts and invitations to the meeting. We had been warned that whites walking through those neighborhoods at night did so at the peril of their lives. There had recently been an ugly race riot and there were still snipers and gangs on the loose who would attack whites indiscriminately. The warning proved to be nonsense. We never met kinder people. Faithe went down one block while I covered another, talking to folks sitting on their front porches while their

168

children shouted, played, and dodged traffic in the streets. Many wanted to discuss the Lord, many wanted prayer.

It proved to be a good revival, the offerings scant but the Spirit again moving abundantly, several dozen coming to fellowship and new life with Jesus.

After that the gospel trail deadened and our future seemed precarious. No one else had come forth with an invitation for me to preach, so Faithe and I drove to Cincinnati to attend a revival being conducted by another evangelist.

We rented a one-room apartment in a venerable rooming house for fourteen dollars a week. All it had was a tiny kitchen, two lumpy beds, and an old couch. While Faithe unpacked, I went to the revival and listened to the evangelist magnify the Lord. When the offering basket was passed I gave sixty-five dollars. *Give, and it shall be given unto you.* Since I believed that the Bible was the holy, inspired Word of God, I hadn't the slightest doubt that the promise of Luke 6:38 would be confirmed.

"I need a little money for groceries," Faithe said when I returned from the service.

I told her we were broke.

"Brian! You didn't lose our last sixty-five dollars!"

"I gave it all to God."

"Did God tell you to do that?"

"No, I did it on my own. I felt it was right."

Faithe said nervously, "We're three thousand miles from home, the rent is due soon, we have a quarter of a tank of gas and nothing to eat."

Out of sheer necessity, we fasted for three days and lived totally on trust in Jesus. He quenched our hunger and helped us make do. The fast ended when a girl Faithe met at the revival gave her seven dollars as a contribution to keep us going. We bought hot dogs and beans, which were as delicious as anything ever served at Belshazzar's table.

That night I went to the prayer tent on the revival grounds and told Jesus, "Lord, we don't know what to do, we just don't know where to go from here. Guide us, Lord, so that we may continue working for you."

169

Then I walked into the meeting and the evangelist, whom I had met briefly, called on me to say a few words. I gave an abbreviated testimony, emphasizing how much Jesus had done in my life. When I finished, I walked down the aisle. People began handing me money—twenties, tens, and fives. When I got outside a man walked up to me, put some money into my hand, and said, "Brian, the Lord told me to give this to you." It was the first hundred-dollar bill I'd ever seen. The freewill offerings came to more than five hundred dollars.

Two ministers had been in the congregation and both invited me to preach. We had a meeting at an independent church in Toledo, Ohio, a ragged, rugged industrial city with one of the meanest Skid Row areas I'd ever seen. The soddenness and boredom of the place, its air of quiet desperation, was relieved only by reading its first-rate, informative daily newspaper, the *Blade,* and the fires I could light for Jesus at church.

Our next meeting in Niagara Falls, New York, was before a Pentecostal congregation which held church in a small theater. Faithe played the organ the first night and I preached to a multitude of . . . eight.

"Eight people!" Faithe said afterwards. "Why are we here?"

"We're here because of one of the first things I read in the Bible while I was in the Hole. "For where two or three are gathered together in My name, there am I in the midst of them," Matthew 18:20 says. Eight or eighty thousand, it doesn't make any difference except that with a crowd of eighty thousand, you can reach many more for Jesus. And remember, He started with only twelve."

We soon had more than a hundred and fifty worshippers coming out nightly, people who heard about a young Canadian preacher who had turned from crime to Christ. The revival became memorable because I was able to lead more than one hundred people to the Lord.

Another who heard about me was Reverend Billy White, who pastored the four-hundred-member Bethesda Temple in Tonawanda, New York, north of Buffalo. We stayed in revival there

170

for two months, unshackling hundreds, preparing a place for them before the Lord.

Pastor White also ministered a church in Toronto, and in preaching there I had my most effective meeting since Kansas City. The Gunder Street church was packed every night, and night after night I told what it meant to walk with the Man. Hippies and straights were coming to the Lord by the score.

In the midst of the revival, Mom flew down from Saskatoon. After the service, she said, "Brian, you're a better preacher than Billy Graham."

I laughed, making allowances for Mom's lack of objectivity. I didn't give a hoot about being a better or worse preacher than America's most famous soul-winner. What mattered is that we were both doing the quintessential work of God, which was winning souls.

By now our Pontiac was so cancerous that it had to be replaced. I put down a hundred dollars on a new Buick with no idea how I would raise the remainder of the money. I left *that* problem to Jesus, and as usual, His blessings flowed. The Toronto meeting became so successful that I was able to pay for the car in two weeks through offerings coupled with a loan from my brother. Our gospel wagon now at least was a lot more reliable and safer as Faithe and I made the next long hop to tiny Metamora, in eastern Indiana. It had a population of only four hundred, but it seemed as if everyone in town was at church.

Miracles poured out in healing services for those with faith. One man's conviction was so great that while I was only half way through my sermon he came running down the aisle, asking Jesus to forgive him for his alcoholism and the rotten life he'd inflicted on himself and his family.

The hum of rubber against concrete continued. East St. Louis again. Then a meeting in greater St. Louis. Kansas City once more. Denver. Salt Lake City. Portland, Oregon. Seattle. Then we crossed into Canada and Faithe decided to remain in Calgary, to resume her church work there and see the boy she was engaged to marry.

Heading out alone for my next meeting in Vancouver, driving over breathtaking mountain passes and through scenic national parks created by a divine architect, I felt I had grown tremendously in the past year as a preacher and in the ways of the Lord. More than ever, I was turned on to Jesus. More than ever, I longed to keep my commitment to Him, and honor my pledge to preach His Word.

The future now was more promising. An invitation to hold a meeting had come all the way from Oklahoma. A minister there had heard about my testimony and thought my message would help his congregation. I planned the trip to Tulsa after the Vancouver revival.

As I slowed down to pay a highway toll charge, I was so overcome with happiness that I was crying.

"What's wrong, son? Is there something I can do for you?" the man in the booth asked.

He looked at me like I had lost my mind when I said, "No, it's only that life is wonderful and beautiful. I'm filled with joy because it's marvelous just being alive." Then, I added, "The most wonderful, beautiful, marvelous thing of all is that I'm not riding alone in this car."

Scratching his head, he glanced at the front and back seat.

Before he phoned for the men with the straitjackets, I began telling him about Jesus. I witnessed to him for a long while, saying finally, "If Jesus was with me in prison, I know He is with me in this car."

He grinned, and I reached for his hand through the window. When we finished praying together, he said, "I think I understand now. Son, this is a lonely job. Do you think Jesus might stop by my booth sometime tonight?"

"He'll be there. You wait and see and watch."

And then I sped on to Vancouver where Jesus had a surprise waiting for me. Her name was Gayle Nash. In less than a year, it would be Mrs. Brian Ruud.

15

Breakthrough

> *Sing praises to God, sing praises: sing praises unto our King, sing praises.*
>
> PSALMS 47:6–7

> *Whoso findeth a wife findeth a good thing, and obtaineth favour of the Lord.*
>
> PROVERBS 18:22

It was Sunday morning, a day speckled with sunshine and heady anticipation.

I was wearing my best suit and manners as I waited outside Christian Center Church for Gayle Nash, our meeting arranged through Faithe, who had dated one of Gayle's brothers. Faithe, saying we would enjoy one another's company and that we'd have much in common, had set up our appointment via telephone calls to both of us.

I recognized Gayle instantly from Faithe's description. She walked toward me, a tall, slim beauty with blonde hair, wearing a white suit and green blouse. I felt the same skin-tingling emotion as David must have experienced when he first saw Abishag, the fairest maiden in the Hebrew empire.

Close up, Gayle was loveliness personified: high cheekbones, luminous brown eyes alive with curiosity, her features crafted perfectly by God who had designed her as He did a rainbow or a wildflower. But there was more than physical beauty to Gayle. There was about her an essence, a purity, a spiritual quality, that I had never sensed in any other girl. A girl such as Gayle must have been the inspiration for Solomon's poetry.

It wasn't love at first sight, it was first-sight adoration.

Gayle was the sort of girl who would be attractive to any man. As we introduced ourselves with more ease than embarrassment, I had no illusions about a lasting relationship. I was certain I didn't have a chance with her.

I learned quickly that candor was one of Gayle's many attributes. "I've heard good and bad things about you," she said forthrightly. "I don't know what to believe. You're a preacher, and that's good. But some people say you shouldn't be a preacher."

"There are a lot of things I shouldn't be. I shouldn't be out of prison. I don't deserve to be a free man. I don't deserve to be standing here talking to the most beautiful girl I've ever seen. But I *do* deserve to be a preacher. Christ called me to evangelize in His name and that's what I'm going to do as long as I have breath. It's the least I can do for the super-cool soul Man who put everything together for me."

"I've never heard Christ referred to as a super-cool soul Man," she laughed infectiously. "But I like the sound of it. Do you always refer to the Lord that way?"

"Much of the time, yes. What's wrong with it?"

"Nothing. Just that more conservative preachers and church people might be shocked, might consider it disrespectful."

"I haven't found that to be true. That's the way I think of Him. And the kids I speak to groove on Him when He's talked about that way. They don't find it shocking or disrespectful. Jesus seems more real to them. If Christ were standing here right now,

174

He wouldn't be shocked. He knows my heart and soul, that the last thing I would do is show an ounce of disrespect to Him."

Strains from the opening hymn of the service wafted out from the sanctuary, and we walked inside. I hoped Gayle and I had something moving between us. She seemed as genuinely interested in me as I was in her.

As the service began, we kept glancing at each other out of the corners of our eyes. We chattered between songs and people were glancing at us with a look that said, "Be quiet, don't you know you're in church?"

I felt the Lord wouldn't mind if Gayle and I left the service. I wanted to get to know her better, and I couldn't wait. "Let's get some breakfast," I suggested.

Over steak and eggs, Gayle told me something of her life. Born in Vancouver, she had four brothers and two sisters.

"My grandfather was a bootlegger," she said, searching my face for disapproval.

I chuckled. "So was I."

"In the evenings Grandfather would go up to the attic and sit for hours with a shotgun on his lap, his ears alert for any unusual sound. He thought that someone he was involved with in his gang of bootleggers was going to kill him. He was a very unpredictable man, disappearing for six months or a year at a time. When he came back he never volunteered an explanation as to where he'd been or why he'd left. I suppose that must have driven my grandmother wild. He died at ninety-three, unsaved."

Gayle's father was Jack Nash, once one of the best known rodeo performers in Canada and the U.S., a major contender for the world's bareback riding championship. He worked at pickup jobs during the Depression until he caught on with the rodeo. In a few years he got tired of it. There was too much drinking and carousing and he knew something was missing in his life.

"One day," Gayle said, "he went to a service at a small Pentecostal country church. He caused such a stir, his whole family was saved, and they called him the 'Converted Cowboy of Saskatchewan.' He quit the rodeo and went to Bible school to grow stronger in Christ. He met Mom there. She's a gentle, sensitive person, who was saved when she was a little girl. After they were married, he became a lay preacher and went into the electrical supply and retail business to support his family."

Gayle had come to Christ when she was six. Reared in a home atmosphere similar to mine, she hadn't rebelled, though she too wasn't permitted to go to movies, dance outside church, or live a worldly life. She'd had her first date when she was sixteen. She and her family lived for Jesus and her childhood had been happy.

Gayle was twenty-three, two years older than me. She'd been out on her own for several years and shared an apartment with a girl friend, holding down a key job as a secretary with a well-known law firm specializing in patents and trademarks. She went to church regularly. Far from a prude, Gayle had been exposed to swinging parties and guys who'd expressed a sexual interest in her. "But that's just not my way," she said with conviction.

"Are you going with anyone special?" I asked.

"I am seeing a great deal of one man."

I didn't care much for that, but, of course, it was understandable.

"Do you plan to marry him?"

"Well, he's proposed."

There was enough of a waver in her answer to give me hope.

Following our first meeting, we became inseparable, swimming, water-skiing, exploring Stanley Park with its gardens and forest trails. Beside a lily-covered lake called Lost Lagoon we kissed for the first time.

Then Gayle came to hear me preach at my one-night revival in the Peach Bowl. "You're cool," she said afterwards.

I had to leave for Tulsa after knowing Gayle only one week. On the long drive, she was seldom out of mind. I wanted to hurry back to her as soon as I could. We hadn't put it into words, but there seemed to be an unspoken understanding that we would be married. Everything between us had clicked. Though a separation would be painful, it was fortunate in that we would have time to see if our initial attraction for each other ripened into love.

One night before going to sleep at a motel along the route, I leafed through the Bible to find out what it had to say about a girl as precious as Gayle. The answer was in Proverbs 31:10–30,

"Who can find a virtuous woman? for her price is far above rubies. Beauty is vain: but a woman that feareth the Lord, she shall be praised."

There was a sudden tug in me to return immediately to Vancouver and propose to Gayle, the biblical personification of a virtuous woman who feared the Lord. Only the knowledge that my life was not my own kept me from acting impulsively. Christ had said to me as He had said to Simon and his brother Andrew in Mark 1:16, "Come ye after me, and I will make you to become fishers of men." My life belonged to Jesus and His work overshadowed everything else, including my yearning to see Gayle. I also steeled myself into accepting my previous realization that the separation would be good for us. Jesus would reunite us in His own good time. For the time being I stayed in touch with Gayle by writing her frequently and phoning occasionally.

The Tulsa revival, scheduled for a camp meeting grounds on the outskirts of the city, had to be postponed because of a mix-up in scheduling. I could, after all, have remained in Vancouver a few months longer.

Nothing else opened up—the path ahead was still strewn with thorns of disappointment and indifference for a nearly anonymous Canadian evangelist. I was so strapped for eating money that I took a temporary job at Dallas' Love Field, one of the world's busiest airports. My work consisted of cleaning and polishing private jets. I spent lunchtime and nights reading the Bible and dreaming of those elusive multitudes among whom I could cast the net of Jesus and fish for souls.

I was staying at the home of a fiercely Christian black woman —Mama Lewis, as she was known to everybody, a walnut-skinned, laughing-eyed militant for Christ. She and her husband treated me like one of their own. "Don't you worry," Mama Lewis said, "God isn't through working miracles for you." This in response to my impatience at having to wait for my next meeting to begin.

When the Tulsa revival finally got under way, the crowds were so thick night after night that I could barely find a parking place.

Scores were delivered from cigarettes and alcohol. A middle-aged bartender poured two bottles of vodka empty at my feet on the platform. "I'm never going to take another drink," said the man who'd been a drunk for fifteen years. He wrote me several years later, declaring that he had kept his nondrinking pledge to God and now was earning twenty-five thousand a year as a salesman.

Young people were set loose from dope, and so many in the congregation wanted prayer for relief from physical illnesses that a long healing line was formed. In Acts 9:15 God commanded His disciple Ananias to heal Saul of Tarsus because "he is a chosen vessel unto me." Ananias laid hands on Saul and restored his eyesight. To those in need of healing, I declared as Jesus did to the woman diseased with an issue of blood in Matthew 9:22, "Thy faith hath made thee whole."

People later testified that they were healed of arthritis, heart trouble and other ailments.

The skeptics, the cynics, the unbelievers without Jesus, the sophisticated and glib who spend much of their lives hopelessly nursing their hang-ups, frustrations and anxieties, many ending up in expensive psychiatric analysis, scoff at the laying on of hands and healing by faith. But the percentage of cure through psychiatry is shockingly low, and half the hospital beds in America are filled with psychiatric leftovers who have not been helped by therapy.

The only psychiatrist with a guaranteed cure is God.

There is no point in lingering long on the age-old argument of whether or not faith and prayer result in healing. The Bible says they do. My own metamorphosis is testimony to the healing power of the living Christ. So are the testimonies of thousands in my files who've been cured of every type of emotional and physical sickness.

By myself, of course, I can heal no one. I can act only as a channel through which the miraculous power of the Lord's healing is conveyed. Though I do not have healing lines as such at all my services, everyone who answers the altar call and gives himself to Jesus is the beneficiary of divine healing—teen-agers who renounce dope, adults who renounce whatever sin is destroying them. They are all made well by Jesus.

Let the skeptics scoff and suffer. Let those drowning in the uncertainties and guesswork of psychiatrists—who, not so incidentally, have the highest suicide rate of any professional group—wonder why they do not find the answers to their problems. Let those who are using methadone instead of heroin wonder why they are still addicted. Methadone does not cure, it merely substitutes one drug for another. Let those who've sought the truth in satanic cults, in witchcraft, in gurus and exotic, mystical eastern religions, in yoga, astrology, tarot cards, in all the black arts which are the Devil's work, wonder why they remain sick, unhappy, still searching, still unfulfilled.

Let those who are in Christ have the sacred, inner knowledge that in the era of hydrogen bombs and man's reaching out to the moon and the planets, Jesus yet works miracles and heals those who are ill in body and mind. As someone has said of divine power and faith, "For those who believe in God, no explanation is necessary. For those who do not believe in God, no explanation is possible."

My calling is to awaken people to the gifts that Jesus has in store for them once they accept Him as ruler of their lives. And that's what I tried to do at my next meeting in Fort Smith, Arkansas, but for a time I thought Jesus had prepared my place in heaven.

One of the many who were saved the first night was an eighteen-year-old girl. She turned off drugs, which infuriated her boyfriend. He walked in stoned the next night with three of his friends, boasting to one of the ushers, "I'm going to kill that evangelist for what he did to my chick. This is going to be his last sermon."

The leaders of the church wanted to call the police. But I said that Jesus would take care of me. Jesus was bigger than four or four thousand murder-bent dudes.

They were sitting near the front, scowling and scornful, as I began my message. I preached directly to them. "All I want is to be your friend. I love you. Jesus loves you." At the end of the sermon all four were on their knees, mainlining with Jesus.

In Fairfax, Oklahoma, population about twenty-five hundred, I began a series of meetings in a small Pentecostal church.

After checking into a motel, I went to a small supermarket.

179

I put my purchases, less than fifteen dollars, on the counter before a middle aged, well-dressed woman at the cash register.

She kept darting glances at me as she bagged my items and then announced, "No charge!"

I assumed she was joking. "If you're giving groceries away, I should really have helped myself," I said lightly.

"I've never done this before. But the moment you walked in, I had a feeling about you. I decided I was going to give you anything you wanted. No, I take that back. It wasn't me that decided. The Lord told me to do it."

Her name was Mrs. Opal Morris, and in addition to the free groceries, she paid my gas and oil bills during the revival and introduced me to dozens of her friends. She is still one of my dearest friends.

Several hundred attended my meetings, and during the day I went all over town, praying, ministering, rapping for hours with believers and nonbelievers. It got so that by the time I left a great many people were calling me the town reverend. All I tried to do was leave a little bit of Jesus everywhere I went in Fairfax.

At Coffeeville, Kansas, I was invited to speak daily on the local radio station. God started moving so powerfully that we couldn't hold the crowds within the confines of the small church where I was preaching. So we moved the revival to a large hall downtown, where every chair was filled for three weeks. One man was healed of a paralyzed leg, another of ulcers, many more of other afflictions. Again people rose and gave unbidden testimonies of how they had been made well during the services, people of faith who were cured of all types of illnesses.

Coffeeville had been an upper for Christ. Joplin, Missouri proved a downer. In a week of meetings, not a single soul made a decision for Jesus. The Devil began gnawing at me again. My nerves began to twitch, my tongue felt dry. "Brian," the Devil said, "what you need is a fix. You'll feel so much better."

To loosen myself from Satan, I decided I would witness to the next stranger I saw. I found myself outside a Christian Science reading room. I went inside and told two of the ladies who happened to be there about the real Christ who had changed my life when everything else had failed. They knelt, joined me in prayer, and declared themselves born-again Christians. I was much happier as I drove to Kansas City, where I preached one night. Then I went back to Dallas and Mama Lewis.

Weeks passed without my accomplishing anything for Jesus. Of the myriad pulpits available in America, none seemed to have room for me. I began talking to the Man, asking Him what was wrong, what He wanted me to do next.

Brian, He answered, *pack your bags and move on.*

His voice was gentle but firm. Still it scared me.

"I've only got thirty-three dollars and you want me to leave? Where do you want me to go?"

There was no reply. I had been commanded, and I had to obey.

While Mama Lewis bustled in the kitchen, I went to my room and packed. When I told her I had to split, she said I should at least stay for supper. I told her, "I think I'd better leave now."

"Is there anything wrong?"

"No, Jesus has told me to go."

"But where? What will you do?"

"I don't know. I only know that I have to do what He asks."

"I understand," Mama Lewis said, giving me a bear hug and kissing me good-bye. I drove down the streets of Dallas, not knowing where to go. Then I noticed Mission Motel. I figured the name was a sign. The room was modest, the most inexpensive I could find. It had just been repaired and repainted after a fire. The smell of smoke was still present.

The next week was long and lonely. I spent seven days doing nothing except fasting, praying, reading the Bible, and hoping. Then I went to Fort Worth, met a pastor, and was allowed to preach a few times. At one meeting a man came up to me and invited me to a large prayer meeting in Dallas

They asked me to testify to a congregation numbering in the hundreds. As I spoke, my body began to tingle, and I was suffused with love and the overwhelming presence of God. I talked for more than an hour and afterwards people came down the aisles, embracing and kissing me. Scores were delivered. One teen-

181

ager told me, "If Christ could do so much for you, I'm sure He can help me." He shook my hand and left in my palm three caps of LSD.

Things began falling into place as Jesus cleared my way to larger meetings in Houston and Dallas. In Shreveport, Louisiana, Life Tabernacle Church sponsored my radio appearances on KEEL, which brought hundreds of teen-agers out to the revival. People of every age and denomination came to Jesus—Baptists, Methodists, Catholics, Nazarenes, and Pentecostals. The Shreveport meeting grew so large that we had to transfer it across the street to the Municipal Auditorium, and five thousand attended the final service.

I decided now to return to Vancouver and Gayle. Eight months had quickly fled and my feeling for her had grown. She had a grip on my heart that was impossible to ignore.

As I drove to Vancouver, I thought of all the revivals I had been fortunate enough to hold through the American South, Southwest, and Middle West. I had seen several thousand come forward to quicken and renew their lives through Jesus. Not only those who had never set foot in a church or had been turned off by religion early in life because the real Christ wasn't explained or interpreted, but tithe-paying members of many churches were blessed with a fresh, exciting personal relationship with Jesus. The door to everlasting life had been opened to them and doors were beginning to open wider for me. My dream of an independent, Christ-centered, interdenominational ministry, unaffiliated with anyone except Jesus, was taking shape and form.

Gayle was even more beautiful than I remembered, both physically and spiritually.

"Brian," she said, and her words came in an inspiring torrent that drowned me in joy, "I want to tell you what's happened to me, the most important thing that's happened in my life. I liked the way you talked about Jesus and wanted to find Him in the same way you had.

"The first Sunday after you left I went to church and listened to some turned-on young people testify. Their eyes sparkled and there was the shine of God on their faces.

"I suddenly knew where I had failed. I had never totally and completely, without reservations, given myself to Christ. I'd read somewhere—and how true it is—that people could never find peace and happiness until they were ready to commit themselves to something worth dying for.

"I decided Christ was that something and I gave myself to Him with all my heart. An unforgettable feeling came over me. I had joy and peace with Christ, and the peace that passes all understanding filled my heart and life to overflowing. I realized that I hadn't grown in grace and knowledge of the Lord, had not built a daily, personal, and real relationship with Christ.

"I had never really known Jesus as Lord of my life. I realized I needed to become fully grounded in the Word of God, absorb and feed upon Him through studying the Bible. I had to show myself approved unto God. That I was no longer a half-hearted Christian, that I would no longer be ashamed or reluctant or fearful of witnessing for Him.

"I felt different. Now I had real goals to strive for. I could at last meet life head-on with purpose and meaning. I found out who I was and why I was on earth. I was needed to fulfill my duty as a follower of Christ, to say 'not my will, Lord, but thine be done,' to be obedient forever to His voice. I discovered that was no longer a task, it was a privilege and honor. I'd found the secret of true happiness and peace of mind.

"Driving home from church, I prayed, 'Lord, use me,' and I experienced a deep awareness that Jesus was sitting next to me. His presence engulfed and surrounded me. From that moment on, I knew my life wasn't my own."

Gayle's eyes and face, as she finished telling me of her soaring rebirth in Christ, sparkled and shone with God. Joined by a common goal, ruled by a Savior we both understood in identical terms, I couldn't hold back a moment longer.

"Gayle, will you marry me?"

"Yes. On one condition."

My heart raced, and my breathing was suspended.

"That the Lord will always come first in our marriage."

"Hallelujah!" I shouted and the other patrons in the restaurant where we were sitting turned and laughed.

183

We set the wedding date and visited Gayle's parents and mine. We received their blessings and approval.

Meanwhile, I continued holding revivals anywhere I could, throughout British Columbia, Toronto, and Seattle. Then I worked with Dad for a while, helping him reorganize his ministry. He'd decided to sell his church and enter the mission field where he could reach more souls.

We were married in Gayle's church the day before her birthday. Gayle was triumphant in white, lovely beyond description. A super-cool preacher recited the holy vows in sight of God. "Brian, my son, my son," Dad said after he married us. "How very, very far you've come."

There wasn't time for a honeymoon as Gayle and I began working side by side for the Lord. "You do the preaching and I'll take care of everything else," Gayle said. That relieved me of much of the detail connected with each revival.

From Vancouver we made it to our next assignment for Jesus in Houston, Texas, after three days of steady driving. I preached at Pastor Gordon Magee's brand-new church, called Elim, named for the fourth stopping place after the Israelites miraculous crossing of the Red Sea.

In that revival we saw more miracles—dopers, alcoholics, and homosexuals set free, those of faith delivered of nervous conditions and physical illnesses.

At the end of the second week of the meeting, the wife of an attorney in whose home we were staying made a bold suggestion —that I should meet kids on their own turf, go directly into schools and speak to them. The drug scene in Houston, as everywhere else, had spread like a holocaust. Parents of the poor, middle class, and wealthy all shared a common problem—the terrifying fear of dealing with their kids who had turned on to drugs or might turn on any day.

Surprisingly, the permission came readily. There were no hairline distinctions made about separation of church and state, which had been a hot issue since the Supreme Court, displaying an incredible lack of wisdom, had outlawed simple, reverent, nondenominational prayers in schools. The opposition I thought might surface did not materialize. Such opposition, however, was to come later in Dallas, causing a raging controversy. But Houston school officials knew they had a massive problem and were desperate to try any solution.

God became the court of last resort.

I went into the schools, not as an evangelist or to hold a service, but only as a peer of the teen-agers to tell them straightforwardly how God was solely responsible for me splitting the drug and crime scene. And what God could do for me, He could do for anyone. No other antidrug cure of any kind was working, although the federal, state, and local governments were sending more than a billion a year down the tubes in gigantically unsuccessful programs to rid America of everything from pot to heroin.

That first day in Houston I spoke in the auditoriums of Stephen F. Austin, Jesse Jones, and Spring Wood High Schools. Approximately twenty-five hundred kids attended my talk at each school.

The response was super-fantastic. Teen-agers came forward voluntarily, asking for prayer, hundreds in all three schools renouncing drugs.

The Lord, although He was barely mentioned, accomplished in each forty-five-minute tell-it-like-it-is talk what all the lectures, secular rap sessions, and parental and establishment disapproval had been unable to accomplish in years.

The church that night was jammed to capacity, and throughout the remainder of the meeting, parades of young people came forward for salvation. The local papers sent reporters. "He held his largely teen-age audience enthralled," the Houston *Post* said.

"With only word of mouth publicity, young Ruud packed the church to overflowing," reported the Houston *Tribune*. "The clean-cut young man—he looks much like Billy Graham must have looked when he was a young man—evidently inspired youthful dope addicts with the confidence that they can kick the habit with divine aid."

I spoke at three Houston schools, and all of them responded with the same enthusiasm.

God had opened a new phase of my ministry, providing a

major breakthrough for me to reach multitudes. I went on to speak at schools in Galveston, Nacodoches, San Antonio, and Corpus Christi, Texas. The schools also opened up in Shreveport, Louisiana.

Unsolicited "To Whom It May Concern" letters of recommendation poured in.

Two typical examples:

"Mr. Brian Ruud spoke to our student assembly," wrote Harmon Watts, principal of Stephan H. Austin High School in Houston. "The message he presented as pertaining to 'Drugs, Drug Addiction, and the Escape to Nowhere' had the greatest impact on our student body of any program we have had at our school in recent years. I highly recommend Mr. Ruud as a speaker and for his contribution to young people. His approach to the subject of narcotics and the permanent escape he has found in his trust in Jesus Christ is most touching and effective."

The letter from Richard Streif, principal of Ball High School in Galveston, said: "It was our privilege to have Brian Ruud appear at two assembly programs. Mr. Ruud was one of the most effective speakers to appear at our school. The student body was attentive to every word. I can heartily recommend to any school the services that Mr. Ruud can offer youngsters today. I feel that the Galveston community has benefited immensely by his appearance."

In San Antonio, I held revivals in several churches. At one meeting, more than nine hundred souls were brought to Christ. While preaching in San Antonio, Texas Governor Preston Smith publicly endorsed my work. The governor also issued a certificate making me an Honorary Texas Citizen. That was quite a prize for a once hung-up ex-con. It was incredible how far Jesus had taken me.

Aside from speaking at schools, I was invited to address two groups of influential Christian businessmen. I also gave my message to a group of young Catholics in a late afternoon meeting. Twenty were saved, including a nun dressed in her habit who for the first time in her life gave herself to Jesus in a personal, direct relationship.

The next stop—Houston—proved to be the big bustout for my ministry for which I had prayed.

When my revival got under way at Reverend Austin Wilkerson's Evangelistic Temple, he said that in the twenty years he had pastored the church he had never seen such crowds and results, particularly among the young. Almost eighty percent of the congregation was under twenty-five. The kids were sitting all over the floor, the platform, in the aisles, even the choir loft was filled. I like to pace while I preach, but the crowd was so large that I had to confine myself to a six-by-three-foot area.

"Counselors report that over 800 teens have accepted Christ during the first week of the crusade," the church newspaper said. "A conservative estimate of 200 have been baptized in the Spirit and literally hundreds have been delivered of smoking and drugs, turning in supplies of cigarettes and narcotics of every description as conviction gripped their hearts."

The city was on fire for God, and remained so for a month. Virtually all of Houston heard how Christ was moving, and the crowds grew larger at every service. Baptists, Episcopalians, Lutherans, Catholics, and Jews, plus members of many other denominations, were filled by the Holy Spirit.

Under a headline, EX-DRUG ADDICT, NOW EVANGELIST, PACKS SANCTUARY, the Houston *Chronicle* gave its version of one meeting—Ruud, "acting much like a Rolling Stone in concert, began talking about Jesus while the youngsters stared and listened. For nearly three hours Ruud performed for Jesus. Hardly a soul squirmed. Before it ended, Ruud had the youngsters standing, praying, singing, laughing and, with upstretched arms, reaching for the Son of God. 'I don't believe any church is going to do anything at all, but the love of Jesus Christ will do everything,' Ruud says. 'When Jesus gets hold of you, the tide turns.' That is his message and he delivers it powerfully.

"Reverend Wilkerson said he took a box containing every conceivable pill and marijuana to Houston narcotics officers following Ruud's talk."

The Houston *Post* added: "During Ruud's stay in the city, hundreds of teen-agers have turned in pounds of marijuana, scores of pep pills, LSD cubes and over a dozen exotic oriental pipes for smoking hashish, an extremely powerful first cousin of marijuana."

Suddenly I was a celebrity for Jesus Christ. On one day alone, I received phone calls from six large churches throughout the country to preach. A reporter-photographer team was sent by *Life* magazine to cover the revival.

Then came Dallas. At first everything went smoothly. I was invited to speak at several schools and the response from the kids was again overwhelming.

All at once an edict went out—banning me from any further school appearances. I knew Jesus didn't want me to accept that passively. I protested politely but insistently on grounds that God should not be expelled from the schools, especially since the consensus among the kids and their folks was that I be allowed to speak. I was doing nothing more sinister than making as valiant an effort as possible to deliver young people from drugs. That hardly seemed a criminal act, and I was flabbergasted at the amount of commotion that resulted.

The dispute and the subsequent lifting of the ban against me was fully reported in a series of stories in the Dallas *Times Herald.*

SCHOOLS ERASE RUUD BAN, BUT CONTROVERSY REMAINS

Dallas school officials have lifted a ban on the appearance of Canadian evangelist Brian Ruud in city schools, but a new controversy has been fanned by teachers.

A move was made Tuesday to have the Classroom Teachers of Dallas serve notice on the school district that the CTD is opposed to sectarian religious indoctrination programs in the public schools.

However, CTD faculty representatives voted by a narrow margin to table the proposal presented by Bruce Hunter of Bryan Adams High.

188

Hunter said his motion grew out of the flap over Ruud's Christian evangelistic approach in presentation of a drug abuse program.

"Some of the teachers were highly offended," Hunter told the *Times Herald*. . . .

Ruud will be permitted to speak at school assembly programs again provided he is invited by the school principals involved, school officials announced. . . .

Ruud, who dresses in a mod style, urges youth to turn on to God rather than drugs. He holds programs in schools and invites students to attend sessions at local sponsoring churches.

"He was making a pitch for religion and it doesn't seem a function of the schools," Hunter asserts.

Hunter said he believes in religion but said Ruud's appearances in assemblies were directed to only one religion.

Teachers supporting efforts to table Hunter's motion argued it would cause some persons to think the CTD is antireligious or antichurch.

Herb Cooke, CTD executive director, issued a statement Tuesday night supporting the viewpoint of Ruud's critics.

SCHOOL DRUG PROGRAMS CENTER OF CONTROVERSY

School Supt. Nolan Estes said Wednesday that he does not regard the mention of God in drug abuse programs in Dallas schools a violation of separation of church and state.

"I'm opposed to indoctrinational programs," Estes said. "But for a speaker to say God helped him get off drugs is not indoctrinational."

The Classroom Teachers of Dallas voted by a narrow margin to table a resolution opposing indoctrinational religious programs.

"If we approve this without a lot of thought
it will look like we are antireligious or
against the Church," said Louis Wittkower.

Bruce Hunter's resolution was prompted by
the appearance of Canadian evangelist Brian
Ruud in several Dallas schools.

"Such programs are based on religious
beliefs diametrically opposed to those held by
others and thereby create an undesired
divisiveness among our students and patrons,"
Hunter claimed.

Estes disagreed, however, saying, "We have some
common moral and spiritual values which we all
agree to and aspire to teach in our schools.

"If you take values out of our classrooms, you are
raising robots who will answer to any master."

Estes was one of three administrators who decided to
lift a ban on Ruud.

RUUD GETS SCHOOL TALK GUIDE
CAN MENTION GOD BUT NOT BIBLE,
CHRIST

Canadian evangelist Brian Ruud may say in school
assemblies God helped him overcome a life of crime
and drug addiction, but he cannot refer to the Bible
and Jesus Christ.

School Superintendent Nolan Estes announced
new guidelines Thursday for the controversial Ruud
if he appears again in Dallas school anti-drug
programs.

One school board member had expressed
concern that Ruud's evangelical approach of urging
students "to get turned on to God and Christ"
may violate laws governing separation of church and
state.

And a surge of letters-to-the-editor and telephone
calls to school officials reflected public interest

in the issue following complaints from teachers that Ruud's program is essentially a religious one.

The Canadian evangelist admits to a life of crime and drug addiction. He tells students that God and Jesus Christ intervened to change him.

Ruud, modly dressed and long-haired, quotes from a Bible in a dramatic and emotional appeal.

Dr. Estes said Thursday, "We have informed him that teaching moral and spiritual values through any form of religion is a violation of our policies. . . .

Estes said Ruud would be permitted to make references to God because "moral and spiritual values are a fundamental part of our democracy."

He ruled references to Christ and the Bible would constitute a sectarian approach and be a violation of laws governing separation of church and state.

The schools, it was pointed out, try not to show favor to Christian religions or other sects since students come from differing religious backgrounds. . . .

School board member Mrs. Henri Bromberg expressed concern that Ruud's program may be a violation of the constitutional requirement for separation of church and state. . . .

Mrs. Bromberg conferred with Estes. The superintendent later said the new guidelines for Ruud should clear up the question.

Most of the letters-to-the-editor have supported Ruud.

"Brian is truly a man of God, and is, as I see him, trying to reach people with the Word," one letter said in Thursday's edition of the *Times Herald*.

I accepted the guidelines issued by the school board. I wasn't interested in hassling anyone except the Devil. I was invited into twenty-two Dallas high schools, many of them several times.

191

Literally thousands of young people swept drugs from their lives, hundreds coming out to the revival to take the further step of giving themselves to Christ.

The issue of separation of church and state became academic as wonder-eyed parents and educators witnessed His life-changing power. He proved time and again that He was the only lasting cure for drugs. A billion dollars a year couldn't match His effectiveness in moving kids from junk to glory and splendor, young people like myself now forever welcome prisoners in the all-cool world of the super-cool soul Man.

God's blueprint for my life from now on became evident. He wanted me to continue spreading His good news everywhere and wanted to see my ministry grow. To achieve that goal He touched the hearts of a number of prominent men who had heard me preach.

I was invited to Dallas, and there The Trip Beyond, Inc. was formed, with headquarters at 334 Centre Street. For a drug freak turned Jesus freak, the list of men who gave their names, time and support to my ministry was enormously imposing: men from a number of professions, not hung up by denominationalism but united by a common love for Jesus.

The officers of The Trip Beyond are Reverend Austin Wilkerson, president; Reverend Paul Morell, pastor of the Tyler Street Methodist Church in Dallas, vice-president; Dr. Warren Greene, Dallas urologist, secretary; Jack R. Hall, vice-president of Furrs, Inc., Lubbock, Texas, treasurer.

Board members are Houston District Judge Wyatt Heard; Harald Bredesen, pastor, Trinity Christian Center, Victoria, B.C.; Dr. Doug Roberts, physician, Victoria, B.C.; Houston Catholic Archbishop John Stanley; Ed Mathews, owner of Early American Builders, Inc., Fort Worth; Rev. Curtis Mitchell, pastor, Christian Center, Surrey, B.C.; Blanchard Amstutz, Crusade Coordinator, the Billy Graham Evangelical Association, Minneapolis; Rev. Charles Jones, pastor, Bethel Temple, Fort Worth; J. H. (Gebo) Heil, owner of Heil Lumber & Construction Co., Humble, Texas; Coy Holdridge, President of H&H Petroleum Corporation of Dallas; Pearl Mathews, Professor, Fort Worth University; Wesley Jamison, President of International Monetary Systems Corp.; Rev. Jack Gray, Evangelist, Tyler Street Methodist Church; Rev. Gene Whitcomb, pastor, First Assembly of God Church, Rockford, Illinois; Amos Watkins, General Superintendent, Hennessee Homes, Inc., Houston; and others.

Tom Wisdom, an ex-alcoholic who was saved at the age of twenty-two and whom I met at a revival, initially assisted with setting up and organizing The Trip Beyond offices and our magazine, *Scenes,* which features news about the entire scope of our ministry.

The formal organization of our ministry in January 1970 was wonderful, thrilling, and unexpected. But my office in Dallas is not where the action is. The action—first, last, and always—is in revival. That's why Gayle and I have continued our nonstop jubilee march for Jesus. I've preached from coast to coast in the United States and Canada, the meetings growing, acceptance of Him who made it all possible for me growing.

The challenge of more breakthroughs for Christ is never-ending.

The scores of thousands who have come to know the real Christ at one of my crusades is the name of the game. I want to give to others what I've received myself. I yearn for an electrifying growth of my ministry so that, if God wills it, millions who are unsaved will come to understand Jesus as the divine dude who works miracles.

I never forget where I was once, and where I am now thanks to Jesus. The words of John 11:25–26 were written for me and the millions of others transformed by Christ: "He that believeth in me, though he were dead, yet shall he live: And whosoever liveth and believeth in me shall never die."

I kept those words in mind during the middle of my sermon on the last night of a recent meeting in Dallas when a huge, bearded dude heaved himself from his back-row seat. In sight of the entire crowd, he headed toward me—a Bowie knife gleaming in his hand.

He came on like Joshua assaulting Jericho. I interrupted my message and waited.

He reached the platform, removed his dark glasses, his brown eyes rolling like a pair of dice. When he was a foot away from me he began to hesitate, unsure what his next move should be.

I heard a couple of screams from the crowd. And then the screams turned to gasps of unbelief as he let the knife drop to the floor. "I'm a member of the Hell's Angels. I'm on heroin," he said, "and I want Jesus."

16

A Closer Walk With Thee

Let us hear the conclusion of
the whole matter: Fear God, and
keep his commandments: for this
is the whole duty of man.

ECCLESIASTES 12:13

"This is an emergency!"

The Spanish-accented voice of the stewardess aboard the Braniff Airways fan jet was close to breaking as we hovered some ten thousand feet over Acapulco, Mexico.

"Please, don't panic," she continued in a tone that indicated she was barely able to take her own counsel.

I bolted from my seat and put my arm around her shoulders. "Everything's going to be all right," I said. "Nothing will happen to this plane." She fought for control, smiling now despite her fear. "Just tell us what's wrong," I said.

The stewardess put the microphone of the loudspeaker to her lips again and gave us the frightening news.

"The pilot has asked me to inform you that we are having trouble with our landing gear. I'm afraid it's very serious. We are returning to the airport. If you are wearing glasses, contact lenses, or jewelry, please remove them. Remove your shoes. Also, those with false teeth, remove them. This is no time for pride. The stewardess will collect these articles shortly. We would appreciate your full cooperation. I repeat, this is an emergency."

There were some sixty-odd passengers aboard, most of them Americans, returning, as we were, from vacation.

Gayle and I had spent five days in Acapulco as the guests of Jack and Shelly Hall, two turned-on saved Christians. Jack is the treasurer of our Trip Beyond ministry, and during my three-week revival in Lubbock, Texas, Gayle and I stayed in their home, where they treated us royally. At the end of the meeting, they'd asked us to be their guests and join them for a brief holiday.

Acapulco had been super-cool. Long days on the white, mica-dotted sands of the palm-fringed beaches toasting ourselves crisp. From our hotel room at night there were spectacular moon-drenched views of the bay and the city. We had toured the shops along the waterfront and explored the narrow streets and curved lanes of the old quarter of town, far removed from the villas of the rich and hotel row. Here poverty-stricken Mexicans lived in ramshackle buildings, a depressing contrast to the wealthy gringos who had made the resort one of the most popular winter playgrounds in the world because of its natural beauty and tropical climate. The temperature varied only a few degrees throughout the year, the average about eighty.

A few hours ago we'd awakened to an orange sun and driven with Jack and Shelly to catch a flight home. We were airborne for about ten minutes when the nervous announcement from the stewardess suddenly and dramatically confronted us with the possibility of meeting Jesus sooner than we had planned.

The pilot now was driving the plane in wide circles, using as much fuel as possible so as to avoid fire and explosion when, inevitably, he would attempt to land.

Back in my seat, I opened my Bible to Matthew 25:35–36. The verses were the story of my life. "For I was hungered, and

196

ye gave me meat: I was thirsty, and ye gave me drink: I was a stranger, and ye took me in: Naked, and ye clothed me: I was sick, and ye visited me: I was in prison, and ye came unto me."

Did Jesus do all that for me to have my life end before my work was completed? Was Gayle's life over before she had a chance to evangelize with me in the name of Jesus for at least another fifty years?

Were the lives of Jack and Shelly to be taken when they still had four young children to raise? Were the lives of all my fellow passengers to be ended because of some stupid landing gear that wouldn't work?

The answers to all my questions were a resounding *no*. I didn't think Jesus was going to let the plane crash.

"We're not going to die," I told Gayle. "Jesus isn't ready for us to come home, not yet."

"Maybe," she answered, "it's our time to go. It's one thing to know you're saved and have eternal life, but it is frightening when you're looking death square in the face, to realize that soon you'll be facing God."

For a few seconds my previous certitude wavered. "Honey, in case Jesus *is* calling us, I want you to know that if I've done anything to hurt you, please forgive me. If anything does happen to this plane, I'll see you in heaven."

The deep southern voice of Jack Hall came earnestly over the loudspeaker.

"Shall we bow in a word of prayer?" he said. "Our God, we know you hear us when we pray and right now, dear Lord, we come to you in our need. We know, God, that you hold the universe in your hand. So we ask you, Father, to protect us, to watch over this plane, and to allow nothing to happen to it that will endanger our lives.

"I pray that if there is someone on this plane that does not know Jesus Christ as his personal Savior, he will accept you now, Lord, into his life.

"Lord, give everyone on this plane the peace that only you can give. Be with the pilot, Lord. Guide his hands when he lands.

May your hands be upon his hands, Lord, and may not one life in this plane be hurt. I ask it in the name which is above every name, the wonderful sweet name of Jesus.

"Amen."

Jack's prayers brought tears to the eyes of many passengers. Others were choking back sobs. One mother clutched her baby so hard it began to cry. Wives and husbands kissed each other. Several people repeatedly made the sign of the cross. And some of the passengers merely stared ahead, hollow-eyed. The prevailing mood was a compound of fear and gloom. But I figured that if by some chance we were going to crash, Jesus would want us to go in revival. And this might be my last chance to preach.

"People," I said, "We've got the same Jesus riding with us in this plane that guided Shadrach, Meshach, and Abednego through the fiery furnace.

"If we crash, that doesn't mean we're going to die. We are God's children. What do we have to fear?

"Nothing. Least of all we don't have to fear death. I don't believe anything will happen to us. Not one hair of one head is even going to be singed.

"Jesus won't let me die and He is not going to let you die, either. Hallelujah. Let's praise God."

An elderly woman leaned over in her seat and said, "Son, doesn't anything scare you?"

I said, "Ma'am, I like excitement. Nine years of my life I walked through hell in crime and drug addiction, thinking that it would provide me with the excitement I needed. But I ended up wasted in the bottom of a prison. It was there that Jesus Christ, the real Christ, entered my life and made me a new person. Death to me only says, you're going to see Jesus, the one you owe your life to. So you see, Ma'am, I have nothing to fear and that's why I'm so excited."

The atmosphere snapped from defeat to victory as pure revival broke out. We shouted, clapped, sang hymns, and had a great time for more than an hour, praising Him all the while, comforted now and confident that He was watching over us.

The revival lasted until the captain's voice broke in from his cockpit speaker.

"We're about to land," he said. "God be with us all."

As previously instructed, we cushioned our heads in our laps with pillows and blankets, and our hands were clasped behind our legs to brace them against the impact.

But with my left hand I reached for Gayle's right hand and held it tightly.

If I was wrong—*Watch therefore: for ye know not what hour your Lord doth come,* Matthew 24:42 said—I wanted to walk through the gates of pearl with Gayle.

As we began to lose altitude rapidly, I remembered the prophecy of the evangelist in Winnipeg.

His words, in my mind's eye, formed themselves into a pattern.

one day
this
young
man is going to preach the Gospel. He is going to
be Canada's
leading
evangelist.
He'll sing
the Word
throughout
America
and the
world and
reach
multitudes.

Now Acapulco rushed beside us. The wheels thunked on the runway.

A moment later, the plane, seagull-smooth, glided to a safe halt.

199

17

The Trip Beyond

In thy presence is fulness of joy; at thy right hand there are pleasures for evermore.

Across the street was Disneyland, one of its principal features an attraction called Tomorrowland.

But I was getting ready to speak about a Tomorrowland that was transcendentally more important.

A few weeks before, unknown to me, one of America's greatest soul-winners, Pastor Ralph Wilkerson, of Christian Center Church in Anaheim, California, had been among the congregation at my revival in Columbus, Ohio. The victories for Christ had been astonishing and God moved Brother Ralph to invite me to hold a meeting at his church that was to last for four solid weeks, the longest crusade since his tabernacle had been founded several years before. On faith, Brother Ralph had led the members of his church to commit $1,125,000 to buy a nightclub-theater called Melodyland. Since then he'd built it into a full-

Gospel, full-service church, the fastest growing in California, if not the world.

The bar had been closed, and the foul-mouthed comedians and nude performers who once pranced across the stage were gone. Melodyland had been renamed and converted to the work of God.

Its theater-in-the-round had become the abiding home of the Lord. Its four thousand seats, ranged round the circular stage, gold spotlights the only illumination, were filled to capacity with seekers of every age as I prepared to praise Jesus on this night in 1971. Thousands had already been won to Christ during the revival, one of the largest and most successful of my ministry. Now I prayed that Jesus would allow me to pour His Spirit into hundreds more.

Such was my mission. The Bible declares in Romans 10:14, "How then shall they call on him in whom they have not believed? and how shall they believe in him of whom they have not heard? and how shall they hear without a preacher?"

Oh, Jesus, I prayed, *help me tonight, give me the words and the power to reach the lost and lonely. Jesus, speak through me so that lives may be renewed through your saving grace. Thank you, Jesus. Thank you for this night of revival, and if it be your will, for all the nights of revival to come.*

The stakes for the throng were enormous, hope replacing hopelessness, life rather than death, heaven instead of hell. The stakes were lives that could be forever changed.

As the music from a gospel rock group shimmered to a close, I went to the immense blue-carpeted platform, long microphone cord in hand, ready to pace and preach for Jesus.

It was time now to trip out on Christ . . . lay your burdens down time . . . saints go marching in time . . . Michael, row the boat ashore to the Jordan time . . . putting your hand in the hand of the Man who calmed the seas time.

It was time to tell the assemblage about the real Christ. It was time for The Trip Beyond.

People, I feel so happy to be alive, to be alive in Jesus.

Jesus loves all of you. Did you know that? Doesn't that give you a wonderful feeling, to realize that the super-cool soul Man who walked the shores of Galilee loves you.

People, are you as happy tonight as I am? You can be.

Folks ask me why I'm so happy. How can an ex-drug addict and pusher, a former convict and gangster, be so excited about life and turned on?

It's Jesus and only Jesus, the true Christ I found while I was rotting in the Hole of Prince Albert Prison. His mercy and forgiveness are the blessings that have allowed me to enjoy and celebrate this life and look forward to life everlasting.

Jesus gave me a life I didn't dream existed. And He can do the same for you.

Listen, people. The Bible tells us to listen in Mark 4:9, "And he said unto them, He that hath ears to hear, let him hear." Tonight I want to give you a road map for your life, a trip you'll never forget, a trip that offers you the only life worth living, the only life worth living today, tomorrow, and forever.

I'm constantly surprised at how many people, famous and obscure, are tired of living and ready to spend eternity in hell. Some of them can't wait to get there. I know—because I couldn't wait to get there myself when I tried to commit suicide.

Brian Epstein, the millionaire dude who created the Beatles, was found dead in his London apartment, victim of an overdose of sleeping pills. Why did he want to die at the age of only thirty-four? Because he put his faith in the Beatles instead of a Book called the Bible.

Recently they buried Jimi Hendrix, one of the biggest rock stars ever. He strangled on his own vomit after dropping nine sleeping pills. He was only twenty-seven, and I understand why he hurried himself to his grave. He didn't know Jesus, and so life was a bummer.

The critics described Janis Joplin as the greatest white rock-blues singer of her generation. She was twenty-seven, too, when she died of an overdose of heroin. Poor Janis . . . poor lonely, lost Janis. She used the talent that God lavished on her to destroy herself. That's what happens when you don't have Jesus.

Brian Jones, one of the original Rolling Stones, didn't have Christ, but he had fame, over one million dollars in the bank, a mansion, a bodyguard, and a Rolls-Royce. He went from pot to LSD, and one night while he was on a trip he went swimming in his pool. He drowned at my age, twenty-five! None of his worldly treasures had made him happy.

In Spokane, Washington, a young man was shot to death by the police after desecrating a Catholic Church, wrecking the altar with a sledgehammer. His Dad said his mind was so warped by LSD that he didn't know what he was doing. Just twenty-one years old, he'd suffered irreversible brain damage from only two LSD trips. He believed Christ was the Devil, and he once went to Jerusalem and stomped on the sepulcher of Christ!

Can you believe it?

An honor student at the University of Utah killed himself and left a note that said: "LSD is bad news. It really is. What acid does is intensify everything. I was screwed up enough without taking acid. It probably just buried me deeper in the hole I was in before I started tripping out."

Back in my hometown I had a friend who preferred drugs to Jesus. One night at the bootlegger's he was drinking screwdrivers and doing speed, all together. He was on one gigantic trip, so freaked out that the bartender asked him to leave. When he refused, the bartender said, "Get out or I'll kill you."

Kill! Kill! Kill! That word kept screaming through his mind. He left, but he was back in half an hour with a sawed-off shotgun. He blew the bartender's head off and woke up in jail. "Man," he said to the guard, "why am I here? Did I get a little drunk last night?"

"You killed a man," the guard told him, "you'll be lucky to get life in prison." He'd been so spaced out he didn't even remember firing the shotgun.

That could have been me—or you, any one of you who's on drugs. My story has a different ending because I found Jesus. Your story can be different if you find Jesus tonight.

In my wife Gayle's hometown of Vancouver, British Columbia, heroin is so heavy that there are now between ten and fifteen thousand addicts. The whole province has a total population of only two million. So, proportionately, that's a higher percentage of heroin freaks than anywhere else in Canada or the States, including New York City. The addicts, the police say, steal a million dollars' worth of goods a week to support their habit, and eighty percent of the freaks are under thirty. Some of them use between five and eight bags a day. Some need as many as thirty.

At California's San Fernando Valley State College, a government commission found that forty percent of the students regularly use pot. One coed estimated that eighty-five percent of the students have tried marijuana and described her school as "typical."

A doctor in New York City says that at least eighty thousand veterans have come back from Vietnam addicted to drugs. "These men," he said, "are experts with guns, knives, and explosives. They've been psychologically conditioned to kill. It's no wonder that our streets and homes aren't safe."

The government's programs to help those GI's before they were discharged didn't work, and they didn't work because the government failed to tell them and show them that they could get clean only through Jesus—and this despite the fact that President Nixon has admitted the only cure for drugs is spiritual.

Speaking of guns, do you realize that according to the FBI, there are 375 million unlicensed guns of every shape and description floating around the United States? The only miracle is that there hasn't yet been a full-scale civil war or even more crime in the United States than there is now.

I'd like to see those 375 million guns traded in for 375 million Bibles.

There are nine million alcoholics in the United States. Three million of them hold down jobs in big business and government. There are 130,000 alcoholics in the armed forces, and the Pentagon says they are costing taxpayers at least $120 million a year in lost working time.

A survey of high school students in Washington, D.C. found that half of them are now substituting booze for pot. They want to be like their dads and moms. That same survey uncovered the fact that more than fifty percent had engaged in premarital intercourse, and thought nothing of it.

Nationwide statistics show that more than 200,000 girls a year under eighteen give birth to illegitimate children. One of the girls at a California high school says, "If you're fifteen and not pregnant, you're a nobody." Illegitimacy has become a status symbol. They wheeled one girl into the delivery room to have her baby. She was thirteen years old, and during the birth she was clutching her teddy bear.

According to the California State Board of Public Health, "Syphilis and gonorrhea are out of control, and the tragedy is that most of the cases are among young people under 25."

In the 1960s, Timothy Leary sounded the clarion call for a generation. "Turn on, tune in, drop out," said this false prophet. Leary ruined his brilliant career at Harvard with that philosophy, and now he's in exile abroad. If he returns to America, he faces a total of twenty-eight years in prison on possession of pot and other charges.

I don't have to tell you any more horror stories. They're on the front page of the newspapers every day. But it doesn't have to be that way for you.

The Bible says in Proverbs 30:11-12, "There is a generation that curseth their father, and doth not bless their mother. There is a generation that are pure in their own eyes, and yet is not washed from their filthiness."

Once I was a member of such a generation. I cursed my father and didn't bless my mother. Now I have the coolest Dad in the whole world, and I did all along without knowing it until Jesus changed my life. And my Mom, my God, my Mom. I thank Jesus for her every day of my life . . . and for her prayers.

Mother's prayers!

Do you know how powerful mother's prayers can be? Mother's prayers can stop wars, bring the world out of its anger. Mother's prayers can save the life of a son or a daughter, as the prayers of my mother saved my life.

This generation can be washed from the filthiness of drugs,

206

booze, unholy sex, and cigarettes only through mothers praying to Jesus, and through the prayers of the sin-ridden joining in prayer with them.

People, I beg you, turn on to Jesus. But He's not just a joy-pop, He's a way of life. With Jesus, there's meaning and purpose to life. The real Christ is a new experience every day. The real Christ is an eternal trip.

Jesus, the resurrected son of God—that's my goal for you tonight.

But most people have a strange idea about heaven. They think heaven is a new car and a country club membership. They think a three-martini lunch is heaven. Heaven to many of you teenagers is turning on. But, hey, man, heroin can only keep you up five hours. Morphine might take you up for eight hours. And then you come crashing back down.

Jesus will take you up *forever.* Isn't that wonderful?

Somebody say amen!

Somebody say hallelujah!

Matthew 7:13–14 declares, "Enter ye in at the strait gate: for wide is the gate, and broad is the way, that leadeth to destruction, and many there be which go in thereat: Because strait is the gate, and narrow is the way, which leadeth unto life, and few there be that find it."

Everybody here is on the broad or the narrow road. If the whole world got saved tonight, that narrow road would be wide enough to take everyone into heaven at one time. The narrow road is wide enough for murderers, gangsters, drug addicts, wide enough for good living people who cheat in business just once in a while, nice people who cheat on their income tax, sneak out to the wrong kind of place, run with the Devil on Saturday night and smile at Jesus on Sunday morning in church.

The Devil lays snares for everyone traveling the broad road. Be sincere, Satan says, and you'll make it. Give to the Red Cross. Help the poor. Tithe. None of those things will get you to heaven. Neither will church membership get you to the abode of Jesus and the angels and guarantee you eternal life. Merely being a member of a church won't get you by those pillars of fire into the throne room of God so you can bow before Him at His throne and walk those golden streets.

The only way you'll get to heaven is to be born again . . . born again! That's why I know I'm going to paradise. When I get there I'm going to shout my way all over Hallelujah Boulevard down to the intersection of Holy Roller and Amen Avenues.

Jesus said to Nicodemus in John 3:3, "Verily, verily I say unto thee, Except a man be born again, he cannot see the kingdom of God." That's the only kind of person God will take, those walking the narrow road, those who've been bought with the blood of Jesus shed on Calvary.

You can't ride the fence. Either you're on the broad road to hell or the narrow road to heaven. The Bible says either you're hot or cold. Jesus isn't interested in anybody who's lukewarm.

In Matthew 18:3 He spelled it out to the disciples: "Verily, I say unto you, Except ye be converted, and become as little children, ye shall not enter into the kingdom of heaven."

Acts 4:12 tells us: "Neither is there salvation in any other: for there is none other name under heaven given among men, whereby we must be saved."

You must be born again, converted, saved, before Jesus can give you eternal life, before you can find peace and joy and love and satisfaction in this life. You have to ask Jesus into your heart, humble yourself before Him, kneel down at the foot of the old rugged cross and let Him cleanse you of sin. Then you'll be on the narrow road to heaven.

When a lot of us get to heaven we're going to be amazed at the number who didn't make it, people who sang about God in church, prayed in the prayer meetings, shouted in the services. We are going to find they never made it.

Why? Because they didn't obey the command of Jesus that they be born again. They never gave their heart and life to Jesus. They never had a personal experience with Him.

The whole world is searching for Christ and doesn't realize it.

I laughed at the prayers of my mother and made fun of my father's sermons. I cursed Christ with every other breath. I trampled Jesus under my feet, spit in His face and laughed at His Word.

And yet because I was born again, He is going to welcome me to heaven.

Nothing will give you what you're looking for except the soul Man of the Bible and believing what is written in the inspired Word of God.

The Bible is God's love letter to mankind. The Book is more powerful than any mortal who ever lived, more powerful than any preacher. There has never been a preacher, Billy Sunday, or Billy Graham, or all the Billies, Dwight Moody, the Wesley Brothers, or Martin Luther who has had the power and the fullness contained in Genesis to Revelation.

The Bible says Jesus is the Alpha and Omega and everything in between. His name is Wonderful, the Scripture says, and He is the Bright and Morning Star. The Bible also calls Jesus the Arm of the Lord, Author and Finisher of our Faith, the Cornerstone, Counsellor, Dayspring, Deliverer, Desire of all Nations, the Door, Faithful, Witness, the First and Last, the Glory of the Lord, the Good Shepherd, Great High Priest, Head of the Church, Heir of All Things, Horn of Salvation, Light of the World, Lord of All.

Jesus is a leader greater than Moses, a king greater than David, a commander greater than Joshua, a philosopher greater than Solomon, a prophet greater than Elisha.

Divinity rests on the brow of Jesus. The winds obey Him. One glance from His eyes and there is no more pain.

Jesus is dominion and power. That's the real Christ, the Jesus I get excited about.

If you're born again, you're going to meet Him in heaven. And is heaven going to be groovy. Amen! When I see the Man I'm going to get so excited I'll praise Him for at least a year before I calm down and begin enjoying my first ten thousand years with Jesus.

I want you to meet that Jesus.

I want you to stop rebelling. My whole trip was rebellion, and it got me nowhere until I came to Christ.

Man, it's all cold and lonely without the soul Man. All a bum trip without Jesus. Tonight you can walk out of here clean and fresh and new. Jesus is the only friend you can count on.

Choose life with Him, no matter who you are or whatever is troubling you. You can be dying of cancer, be blind, crippled, wasted on drugs or alcohol.

In Jesus, disease and death no longer matter. Give yourself to Him, and Jesus will answer your prayers. He will say to you as He said to the diseased woman who touched His garment, *Be of good comfort; thy faith hath made thee whole.*

People, remember John 3:16, "For God so loved the world, that He gave his only begotten Son, that whoever believeth in him should not perish, but have everlasting life."

Jesus, I pray that everyone here tonight who wants salvation will come to you, stepping out with the faith that moves mountains.

Accept them, Jesus. In your holy name. Amen.

The hundreds who stream to the altar have accepted Christ's personal invitation, "Behold, I stand at the door and knock: if any man hear my voice, and open the door, I will come in to him, and will sup with him, and he with me."

Changed lives, hundreds of lives changed forever as the burdens lift for the new creatures in Christ.

Among them a Catholic couple who accepts Jesus as their personal Savior.

"Jesus, I've never prayed before in my life," says a man in his forties, a new light beginning to shine in his face. "I've never prayed for my daughter who is kneeling with me now, Jesus. She's fifteen years old and pregnant and unmarried, and I know she's taking drugs. Help us, dear Lord, to find the right road together."

As I walk among the afflicted who have come for salvation, a smiling twenty-seven-year-old dude says he's on the run from a motorcycle gang who wants to kill him. "I'm not afraid now. I've got Jesus, and I'm safe."

"I'm sixty-two years old, Jesus, and I've been miserable all my life. I've never found anything worth living for until now. Jesus, here's my life, what's left of it. I want to walk the last mile with you, Lord."

210

Two teen-age girls with fresh needle tracks lacing their arms give me their heroin. Other young people turn in the Devil's spawn of pills, hashish, joints, and cocaine.

Hundreds of every age renouncing sin for a fresh start with Him, hundreds who have joined me with the real Christ on The Trip Beyond.